RAF Transport Aircraft

CHRIS GIBSON

KEY
Books

MODERN MILITARY AIRCRAFT SERIES, VOLUME 6

Front cover image: In service for over half of the RAF's existence, the Lockheed C-130 epitomises the modern tactical transport. Hercules C4 ZH871, on a low-level navigation exercise, winds its way along a valley in the Mach Loop. (Peter Edwards)

Back cover image: Resplendent in invasion stripes, Dakota ZA947 of the RAF Battle of Britain Memorial Flight takes to the air. Almost 2,000 Dakotas served with the RAF and ZA947 is a tribute to the personnel who served on the type during World War Two and beyond. (MOD/Open Government Licence)

Title page image: Resplendent in Transport Command's white over silver colour scheme, with the lightning bolt cheatline, de Havilland Comet C2 XK671 strikes a pose above the fields of southern England. When the Comets were in service, the RAF transport fleet was at its zenith. (Blue Envoy Collection)

Contents page image: The 1,398ft (426m) Rock of Gibraltar provides a suitable backdrop for Atlas C1 XM407 on the ramp at RAF Gibraltar. An important staging post for Britain's armed forces since the early 1700s, Gibraltar, like Malta, has been key to moving personnel and materiel to the east. (MOD/Open Government Licence)

Published by Key Books
An imprint of Key Publishing Ltd
PO Box 100
Stamford
Lincs PE19 1XQ

www.keypublishing.com

The right of Chris Gibson to be identified as the author of this book has been asserted in accordance with the Copyright, Designs and Patents Act 1988 Sections 77 and 78.

Copyright © Chris Gibson, 2021

ISBN 978 1 80282 185 7

Typeset by SJmagic DESIGN SERVICES, India.

Acknowledgements
Producing a book such as *RAF Transport Aircraft* requires teamwork, but certain individuals deserve a special mention. Peter Edwards kindly allowed use of his original photography from the hills and valleys of Wales, while the photo libraries of Phil Butler, Vic Flintham and Terry Panopalis bring the text to life. Many thanks to Jessica Brown for editing my text and, as ever, the production team at Key Publishing who provided excellent support and advice throughout.

Contents

From Millstones to Mastiffs

*In practice the transport forces are never doing what they are planned to do; unexpected
demands are always arising and for many weeks in every year a number of aircraft
are standing by for emergency operations that in fact never arise.*

Brief for the Chief of the Air Staff, 15 January 1957

Modern society cannot function without logistics, the capacity to provide the necessities of
life where required and at the right time. Military logistics was probably best summed up
by the Confederate States Army's Lieutenant General Nathan Bedford Forest, who, when
asked about his wartime successes, replied, 'I got there first, with the most men.' That is essentially the
function of an armed force's transport organisation, be it by air, land or sea – to ensure personnel and
equipment are in the right place at the right time.

As warfare became increasingly mechanised in the late 19th and into the 20th century, large-scale
campaigns could not be supported locally. French and British forces in the Crimea from 1853 to 1856

**Possibly the first transport aircraft type in British service was the BE.2c of the Royal Flying Corps (RFC). These,
plus Farmans from the Royal Naval Air Service (RNAS), flew food, ammunition, and other equipment (including
millstones) to the garrison at Kut. (Via Vic Flintham)**

were supported by shipping, while the American railway network, and its destruction by each side, played a key role in the American Civil War of 1861 to 1865.

By the outbreak of war in Europe in August 1914, the ship and the train provided mass movement of men and materiel to the front line and, within two years, the scale of operations on the Western Front required a massive logistics 'tail' to support the 'teeth' at the front. By 1917, that tail had extended across the Atlantic to include the United States, in support of the Western powers, and its own expeditionary force. The internal combustion engine, which revolutionised life in the 20th century, provided lightweight power for trucks and, more relevant to this work, aircraft.

The Great War was not a solely European affair, with some of the earliest battles of the war taking place in Mesopotamia (modern day Iraq). As the European powers mobilised their troops by ship and train, British Empire forces moved to protect oil installations from falling into the hands of the Ottoman Empire, which was aligned with the Central Powers (Germany and the Austro-Hungarian Empire). The Royal Navy had recently converted its ships from coal to oil burning, so protection of this valuable commodity was key to successful war fighting.

What has the Royal Navy's fuel supply got to do with RAF transport aircraft? Nothing actually, as the RAF did not come into existence until 1918. Therefore, it was the Royal Flying Corps (RFC) and Royal

In the later stages of the Great War, particularly as Allied troops rapidly advanced in the Hundred Days Offensive, aircraft from the newly created Royal Air Force supported troops by delivering supplies. Aircraft such as the Royal Aircraft Factory R.E.8 dropped food and ammunition to the troops as they advanced beyond their supply lines. (Via Phil Butler)

Naval Air Service (RNAS) that were involved in the operations in Mesopotamia. One significant event that involved aircraft in the Mesopotamian campaign was the siege of Kut, where a British Empire garrison was besieged from 7 December 1915. Kut-al-Amara is 100 miles (160km) south of Baghdad, and as the siege continued into the spring of 1916, the RFC and RNAS conducted the first military supply missions by air.

From the beginning of April 1916, Royal Aircraft Factory BE.2c aircraft from 30 Sqn RFC, plus RNAS Farmans and seaplanes, delivered food and ammunition to the garrison, and amongst the stores was a set of millstones, possibly the first piece of support equipment ever delivered by air. Despite several attempts to lift the siege, the garrison surrendered on 29 April 1916, with 13,000 troops taken prisoner.

Almost a century later, British troops were again in action in the same area, now Iraq, and the British forces were supported by RAF aircraft such as Boeing C-17A Globemasters that delivered equipment like Mastiff protected patrol vehicles. In that century, the RAF has embraced every innovation in military transport aircraft and pioneered many of the techniques in use today. *RAF Transport Aircraft* will describe the aircraft that have met Britain's armed forces' airlift needs from the millstones of 1916 to the Mastiffs of 2006 and beyond.

A Force Protection, Inc. Mastiff protected patrol vehicle being loaded into an RAF Boeing C-17A Globemaster. The 90 years that separated delivering millstones and Mastiffs saw transport aircraft lift capacity increase two thousand-fold. The handling of loads has similarly improved. (MOD/Open Government Licence)

Chapter 1

Never at Peace

Many military units have claimed to be the first in and last out of various campaigns. But the truth is that it is nearly always air transport that can truly lay claim to this honour.

Group Captain Richard Bates, 'The Evolution of Air Transport',
RAF Historical Society seminar, October 1999

Before the establishment of a dedicated command to oversee and co-ordinate its transport effort, the RAF saw little need for such an organisation. That all changed during World War Two when thousands of aircraft had to be moved from the 'Arsenal of Democracy' in the United States to the United Kingdom, and thence onward to the front lines. The RAF had established the Atlantic Ferry Organisation in July 1940, and a year later, on 20 July 1941, RAF Ferry Command was set up. Renamed Transport Command in March 1943, the command operated around the world and became a key asset in the war against the Axis Powers.

Never at peace. Hercules XV217 and XV176 from XXIV Sqn operating from the forward base at Bhairawa in Nepal to provide famine relief during Operation *Khana Cascade* in February–March 1973. The operation was necessary because of crop failure, and over 2,000 tons of rice and grain was delivered by the Hercules detachment. (Blue Envoy Collection)

Post-war Transport Command provided tactical and strategic airlift for all the services and was renamed on 1 August 1967 with the somewhat more apt Air Support Command. These titles only lasted five years on the RAF's transport aircraft, as the separate Air Support Command was absorbed into the Strike Command structure in September 1972.

Transport aircraft, certainly those of a nation with modern armed forces, are always engaged on operations, always busy doing something. Never at peace.

What Is a Transport Aircraft?

Generally speaking, a transport aircraft is a military aircraft, while a cargo aircraft is civil. That line may be blurred when it comes to modern multi-role types such as the Airbus Voyager, but this was not always the case. Essentially, modern civil cargo aircraft carry neatly palletised freight tailored to fit the converted airliner's cabin and cargo holds, whereas a transport aircraft has a large door at one, or both ends, of the fuselage and the freight can be driven straight in.

The first thing to remember about military transport aircraft is that whether there is a war on or not, they are always in action, as there are always personnel and materiel to move. Fighting a modern war needs air transport and a Typhoon unit deploying to Cyprus to conduct operations over Iraq or Syria, as Operation *Shader* requires support staff and equipment. The most efficient way to move them is by air and if your transport has tanker capability, as in the Voyager, even better.

End-loading is pivotal to the rapid and simplified operation of military transports. An Army Air Corps Lynx awaits loading into the cabin of a Hercules C1 through the large rear cargo doors. (Blue Envoy Collection)

The key to a tactical transport aircraft is a rugged high-flotation undercarriage, such as that used on the C-130J. An RAF engineer checks the tyre pressures on a Hercules. (MOD/Open Government Licence)

The Falklands conflict showed how important transport aircraft, particularly the strategic transport and tanker/transport, were for the RAF. This view of Wideawake Airfield on Ascension Island probably dates from 1985 due to the presence of a TriStar KC1, ZD948. Also in the photo are a VC10 C1, two Victor K2s and six Hercules C1Ps, including two C(K)1Ps, XV203 and XV213. (Blue Envoy Collection)

Chapter 2
Origins

The tribes of the North-West Frontier of India however remain as heretofore an unsolved problem.
Government of India's own *Official History of Operations on the NW Frontier of India 1920–1935*, published in 1945

The Biplane Era

The siege of Kut was, by no means, the only example of air supply of troops on the ground. During the Hundred Days Offensive in the summer of 1918, Allied troops who had advanced beyond their ground logistics support were supplied with food and ammunition dropped by parachute by RAF (formed in April 1918) aircraft, such as the R.E.8.

After the Great War, the RAF appeared to have little or no interest in transports, and it was left to the aircraft companies and civil airlines to develop aircraft, usually modified bombers, such as the Handley Page 0/400 and de Havilland DH.10, to carry passengers and mail. Being designed as bombers, they were unsuited for carrying freight, never mind passengers. However, one type, the Vickers FB.27 Vimy, was converted to an airliner by fitting a new large, circular cross-section fuselage to become the Vimy Commercial. This interested the RAF, and 55 examples were acquired as the Vickers Vernon, entering

The Vimy Commercial became known as the Vickers Vernon when it entered RAF service in 1921. This example, J7143, was ordered as a Vimy Ambulance but once in service became a Vernon and served with 45 Sqn. (Via Vic Flintham)

service in late 1921, and capable of carrying up to 12 troops or over 2,000lb (907kg) of freight. Vernons were powered by either the Napier Lion, rated at 450hp (340kW) or Rolls-Royce Eagle VIII, rated at 300hp (224kW).

In what has been described as the first airlift of troops in history, in February 1923, Vernons of 70 Sqn and 45 Sqn carried 500 troops to the Iraqi city of Kirkuk to eject Kurdish forces that had occupied the city. The Vernon, thanks to its origins, could also carry out bombing missions, with units operating the type being designated 'Bomber-Transport' squadrons from 1931.

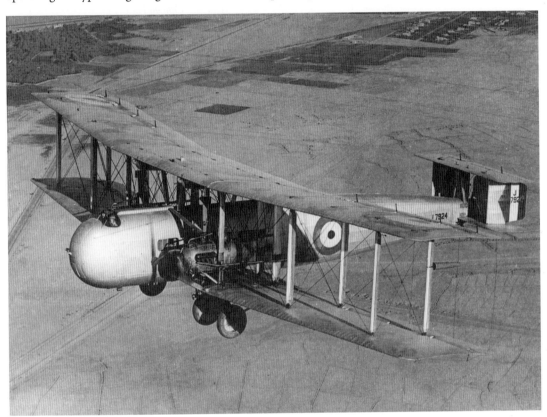

Above: The long career of the Vickers Victoria, especially if the conversions of Valentias are considered, may seem unremarkable by today's standards. In an era when aviation was progressing rapidly, to serve from 1922 until 1944 (the Valentias) is quite remarkable. Victoria III J7294 of LXX Sqn is powered by Napier Lion engines. (Blue Envoy Collection)

Right: The DH.4A transport version of the Airco DH.4 bomber featured a cabin for two passengers aft of the pilot. This DH4A, F5764, was on the strength of 1 Comms Sqn and based at Kenley during 1919. (Via Vic Flintham)

A replacement for the Vernon came in the form of the Vickers Type 56 Victoria, which, despite sharing the Vernon's configuration, was bigger, with a 20ft (6.1m) increase in wingspan over the Vernon by using the wing from the Vickers Virginia bomber and employed metal construction. Despite being powered by the same Napier Lion II engines – rated at 450hp (340kW) – as the Vernon, the Victoria could carry 22 troops and replaced the Vernon from 1927. The Victoria is most famous for its use in the evacuation of Kabul in December 1928, when 586 civilians were airlifted to safety in India. History repeated itself with Operation *Pitting*, the evacuation of Kabul during August 2021 with C-17s in place of Victorias. *Plus ça change.*

The last of the Victorias, the Mk.VI, was fitted with Bristol Pegasus air-cooled radials rated at 650hp (480kW). The Mk.VI formed the basis of the Vickers Type 264 Valentia to meet Specification 30/34, which replaced the Victoria from 1934. The Valentia featured a strengthened airframe and new undercarriage featuring brakes(!) and a tailwheel instead of a skid. The 28 new-build Valentias were supplemented by 54 converted from Victorias as the Type 278. Valentias had a somewhat audacious war record during World War Two, being used as night bombers by the RAF in the Western Desert and by the South African Air Force in the East African campaign of 1940–41. Their finest hour came in the May 1941 siege of RAF Habbaniya that followed a coup d'état in late April 1941. Having been surrounded and besieged by Iraqi troops and light armour, supported by German and Italian aircraft, British ground troops and RAF aircraft, including the venerable Valentias of 31 Sqn, attacked Iraqi forces and soon took the initiative. The rebel forces were soon defeated, and the status quo ante restored, although Iraq remained under British control until 1947.

Surprisingly, the last Valentias were finally withdrawn in 1944, having been operated by 31 Sqn and the Communications Flight, Iraq. The Vimy/Vernon/Victoria/Valentia line was operated by the RAF

The RAF had experimented with parachute troops during the 1920s and 1930s. This Vickers Virginia attached to the Parachute Testing Unit at Henlow is demonstrating parachutist delivery, with the parachutist deployed from the port wing. The Virginia bomber, first flown in 1922, was the basis of the Victoria and Valentia transports. (Via Vic Flintham)

The Vickers Valentia soldiered on until 1944 in the Middle East. Most Valentias were upgraded Victoria VIs, identifiable by their tail wheel rather than the skid used on the Victoria. Valentia K-3612 is seen over a city in the Middle East or the North-West Frontier. (Blue Envoy Collection)

for over 20 years, and the types were key players in some of the more interesting aspects of air force operations in the Middle East and India.

Handley Page Aircraft at Cricklewood had developed the largest Allied Powers aircraft of the Great War, in the shape of the four-engined V/1500. However, its predecessor, the twin-engined O/400, became a civil transport aircraft that was operated by Handley Page Transport which, by 1924, had merged with another three airlines to form Imperial Airways, operating large landplanes, such as the HP.42, and flying boats to connect the empire.

The next bomber the RAF acquired from Handley Page was the HP.24 Hyderabad, designed to meet Specification 31/22. It was the last all-wooden bomber in RAF service and the first bomber with Handley Page leading-edge slats. Powered by two Napier Lion V engines, the Hyderabad operated as a bomber until 1933, albeit with reserve squadrons. Originally a re-engined Hyderabad, the HP.33 Hinaidi I was to meet Specification 13/29 for a bomber and powered by a pair of Bristol Jupiter VIII radials rated at 460hp (343kW) rather than Napier Lions, while the HP.36 Hinaidi II was of all-metal construction.

Handley Page Hyderabad J8321 from 503 Sqn flying over Lincoln Cathedral in 1930. Designed as a bomber, the Hyderabad and its successor, the all-metal Hinaidi, were used as transports. The Hinaidi was one of the many types used in the Kabul airlift of 1929. (Via Vic Flintham)

The Hinaidi entered service as a bomber in 1929, but most examples served in the transport rather than bomber role in India, and the type took part in the Kabul airlift of 1929. The Hinaidi II's use as a transport led to the RAF acquiring the HP.33 Handley Page Clive I, which combined the wooden wings and tail surfaces of Hinaidi I bomber with the fuselage of the W.10 airliner. The Clive I could carry 17 troops or around 4,000lb (1,814kg) of freight. The later Clive II was of all-metal construction, with a number converted from Hinaidi II bombers.

By the early 1930s, the writing was on the wall for the biplane, in all fields of aviation. New requirements were issued for monoplanes using new construction techniques for all-metal airframes with increasingly powerful engines. The bespoke transport was still very much a civil type, as the bomber-transport concept was seen to provide an efficient war-fighting air force. All they needed was updating.

The Bespoke Bomber-Transports

The use of the Vickers transports as bombers and the subsequent development of the bomber-transport was very much the brainchild of the commander of 41 Sqn, one Sqn Ldr Arthur Harris. On being appointed commander in 1922, Harris took the view that if an aircraft could lift a ton, that could be bombs or freight, so why not operate them as bombers? Having ordered holes cut in the noses of the squadron's Vernons, Harris had High Altitude Drift Sights installed and sent his crews off to the bombing range. The results were good, so good that the Vernons of 70 Sqn were similarly converted, and the Vernon 'bombers' operated in both roles, as did their Victoria and Valentia replacements.

While the Vickers types could be described as 'accidental' bombers, their ultimate replacement was designed to meet an Air Staff specification, C.26/31, issued in 1931. The type was to be an all-metal cantilever monoplane to carry 24 troops or equivalent in freight in the transport role or 2,000lb (907kg) of bombs, specifically eight 250lb (113kg) bombs, carried on ventral racks. Nose and tail turrets for defensive guns were required, plus a bomb aimer's position in the nose.

Three designs were selected for a 'fly-off': the Bristol Type 130 and Handley Page HP.51 were high-wing monoplanes, while the Armstrong Whitworth AW.23 featured a low wing. The Bristol Type 130 was powered by the proven Bristol Pegasus engine, rated at 690hp (514kW), but the other designs were powered by the Armstrong Siddeley Tiger engine, rated at 750hp (559kW). Delays with the Tiger had a knock-on effect on the AW.23 and HP.51 development programmes, with the latter re-engined with the Pegasus, and ultimately the Bristol type was selected.

The Type 130 entered service in September 1939 as the Bombay Mk.I, powered by the Bristol Pegasus XXII, rated at 1,010hp (750kW). The type was mainly operated in the Middle East, but 271 Sqn used its Bombays to carry supplies for the British Expeditionary Force in France during 1940.

Like its predecessors, the Bombay had a colourful service history, as it saw action when used as a bomber against Italian forces in the Western Desert and Somaliland. The standard fit of rack-mounted bombs was supplemented by explosive charges thrown out of the doors by the crew! The Bombay also took part in operations in Iraq mentioned above, ferrying troops in support of Dominion, United Kingdom and Empire (DUKE) forces. Bombays were modified to deliver parachutists and the first mission of the newly formed Special Air Service (SAS) saw personnel airdropped from five Bombays to attack five German airfields.

Oddly enough, the Handley Page type, dismissed in favour of the Bombay, entered service well before the Bombay, albeit as the HP.54 Harrow bomber. The Harrow had been a stopgap, with its specification, B.29/35, written around the aircraft's capabilities as they stood in 1935 with an internal bombload of 3,000lb (1,361kg). The Harrow's bomber career was effectively ended in late 1939, as the

Right: The archetypal bomber-transport was the Bristol Bombay, but a lengthy development period, and the loss of K-3583, meant it did not enter service until 1939. Outclassed as a bomber in Europe, most Bombays served in the Middle East. (Blue Envoy Collection)

Below: The bomber-transport was probably more bomber than transport, thanks to the defensive armament. HP Harrow K6933 shows mock-ups of the type's rear and dorsal turrets. Also of note is the size of the Harrow, with the figure under the wing lending scale. Of course, he could be a schoolboy! (Via Vic Flintham)

newer purpose-designed bombers, such as the Armstrong Whitworth Whitley, Vickers Wellington and Handley Page Hampden, came on the scene. The type reverted to its original transport role of the HP.51, and some Harrows had their turrets replaced with streamlined fairings, becoming known colloquially as 'Sparrows' (a contraction of 'Streamlined Harrows').

Two variants were built, differing in their engines, with the Harrow I fitted with the Bristol Pegasus X, rated at 830hp (620kW), while the Harrow II was powered by a pair of Pegasus XXs, rated at 925hp (690kW). Of the 100 Harrows built, 81 were the Mk.II. The Harrow continued to serve in a variety of transport roles such as spares delivery and, later in the war, as an ambulance (now known as casualty evacuation) aircraft that could carry 12 stretcher cases or 20 'walking wounded'. The last of the Harrows were withdrawn from service in May 1945.

Harrows served as transports and ambulances until after the war, with the last being retired in 1945. This Harrow of 271 Sqn is being used as an ambulance and shows the fairing where the dorsal turret had been and the structure that replaced the tail turret. Also of note is the glazing along the passenger cabin. (Via Vic Flintham)

The Handley Page HP.54 Harrow served throughout World War Two as transports. Harrows that had their turrets removed were known as 'Sparrows' – Streamlined Harrows – thanks to the new nose. This example, K7011B of 271 Sqn, was lost with all on board on a flight from RAF Portreath in Cornwall to Gibraltar. (Via Vic Flintham)

	BE.2c		
		Vickers Vernon	
Handley Page Hinaidi			
	Vickers Victoria		
		Vickers Valentia	
		Handley Page Harrow	
		Bristol Bombay	
1910	1920	1930	1940

The early days of the RAF transport force saw derivatives of Vickers and Handley Page biplane bombers span three decades during a period of rapid advances in aviation. (Author)

Chapter 3

Transports Go to War

In the last two years of the war the command had more than fulfilled the commitments inherent in its motto
'Ferio Ferendo': what is more the 'truckie' had been born.

Group Captain Toby Stephens, *RAF Historical Society Journal*, issue 22, 2000

Pressed into Service

On the outbreak of war in September 1939, much of the United Kingdom's air transport and civil aircraft were impressed into military service. The British Airways Ltd and Imperial Airways fleets, including types such as the Handley Page HP.42 and the Short C-class flying boats, gained camouflage schemes and RAF markings and were set to work supporting the British armed forces. By the end of November 1939, the two airlines merged to form the British Overseas Airways Corporation (BOAC).

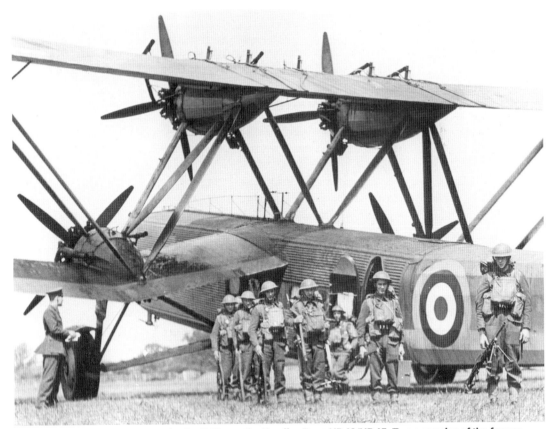

Another airliner pressed into service in 1939 was the Handley Page HP.42/HP.45. Two examples of the former (*Hadrian* and *Horsa*) and one of the latter (*Helena*) were taken into RAF service, but all had been destroyed or damaged beyond repair by late 1940. A section of infantry has just disembarked from a camouflaged HP.42 in early 1940. (Blue Envoy Collection)

Few of these civil types were suited to the military transport role, or even as passenger transports, and were soon replaced with American types, such as the Lockheed 14 Super Electra and Boeing 314A Clipper flying boats. Eight of the Lockheed 14s Super Electras were used by 267 Sqn in the Middle East, while others remained with BOAC and were famously used on the 'Ball-bearing Run' to and from Stockholm, but, from 1943, were superseded by de Havilland Mosquitos in

Soon after the war started, 267 Sqn operated a variety of civilian types from Heliopolis, in Egypt, in the communications role. By 1942, the squadron was operating the Lockheed Hudson VI, four of which are seen over the Western Desert. (Via Vic Flintham)

One of the many airliners pressed into RAF service at the start of the war was the Armstrong Whitworth Ensign, which was operated by BOAC for the duration of the war. Like the other Ensigns, G-ADSR *Ensign* was camouflaged and initially operated between Heston and Le Bourget and then used by BOAC on its routes to Africa and India. (Blue Envoy Collection)

BOAC livery. The Consolidated LB-30 Liberators were used by the Return Ferry Service, flying pilots back to the US and Canada, having ferried aircraft across the Atlantic. One Liberator, named *Commando*, was modified for use by Prime Minister Winston Churchill for trips to meet his generals and Allied leaders. (See Chapter 10)

RAF Ferry Command used converted Consolidated LB-30 Liberators, such as C.I AM920, to return ferry pilots to Canada. AM920 was also used by BOAC as G-AHYB and carried out BOAC's 2,000th crossing of the Atlantic in February 1946. Of note on the C.I are the large windows in the passenger compartment. (Blue Envoy Collection)

Another type operated by 267 Sqn and its predecessor, the Communications Unit at RAF Heliopolis, was the Lockheed 10 Electra. The Electras were also pressed into RAF service at the start of the war and were soon at work ferrying personnel. (Via Vic Flintham)

Enter the Dakota

In addition to the bomber-transports and impressed aircraft, the RAF's transport fleet in World War Two became increasingly reliant on US types, particularly the Douglas C-47 Skytrain and C-53 Skytrooper, known in British service as the Dakota, and converted Consolidated B-24 Liberators. There was yet another source of transport aircraft available to the RAF in the war years, and again this involved bombers.

The burgeoning number, and scale, of airborne operations from 1941 required ever-increasing numbers of aircraft capable of delivering men and equipment, but not all were entirely suited to the role. The bomber/transport, having been designed in the 1930s before the British had seriously examined what is now called 'vertical envelopment', was found wanting in many ways.

As Bomber Command's offensive against Germany gained momentum from 1942, the RAF soon realised that many of the bomber aircraft that had been ordered in the mid-1930s and first two years of the war were not entirely suitable for operations over Germany. While effectively obsolete as bombers, they could be used in the transport role. Converted bombers, such as the Armstrong Whitworth Whitley, were used to deliver paratroops, but they could only carry ten paratroopers, who 'jumped' through a hole in the aircraft floor previously filled by a ventral turret. This was not conducive to rapid delivery of paratroopers, leading to excessive scattering of the troops when they landed, not to mention the sore heads from the unfortunate troops 'ringing the bell' as their heads hit the lip of the hatch. Rapid egress from the aircraft is a key first step in any airborne operation.

Another bomber pressed into service as a transport was the Vickers Wellington, which had a diverse career that ranged from airborne early warning radar test bed, through bomber and anti-submarine

Just under 2,000 examples of the Douglas C-47 – Dakota to the British – served with the RAF in World War Two. These were supplied under Lend-Lease and therefore had to be disposed of at the end of the war. Dakota KN645 was one of the few retained and is on display at the RAF Museum at Cosford. (Terry Panopalis Collection)

As well as being converted to General Reconnaissance as the GR.VI and Air-Sea Rescue as the ASR.V, the Warwick was converted to a cargo transport. In this role, it was fitted with a large ventral pannier to become the C.III, with this example, HG248, powered by the Napier Sabre engine. (Blue Envoy Collection)

aircraft to transport. As with the Bombay and Harrow, the B.9/32 specification for the Wellington originally stated that 18 troops could be carried, so as the Wellington fleet was relieved of bombing duties, Transport Command came calling. Many of the Wellingtons were modified in the field, with Wellington IC bombers having their bomb doors sealed and armament removed to become Wellington XVs and XVIs. These were used extensively in the Middle East, but it was not until later in the war that they saw service around the UK and liberated Europe.

The Wellington's intended successor was the Vickers Warwick and, although it did not enter service as a bomber, it did serve as an anti-submarine and air-sea rescue aircraft and, of relevance here, a transport. The type's non-appearance on the strength of Bomber Command was down to problems with the Napier Sabre engine, which delayed the Warwick to such an extent that it was effectively obsolete as a bomber for use against Germany when it was cleared for service. With a change of engine to the Pratt & Whitney Double Wasp, the type was developed as air-sea rescue (ASR.V) and general reconnaissance (GR.VI) types, but a transport and glider tug variant was also developed. In 1942, BOAC ordered 14 examples for use as mail, freight and passenger transports on the Bathurst (now Banjul) to Cairo route across Africa. Designated Warwick C.I, the Warwicks were, like the Wellingtons, stripped of military kit and fitted with windows, passenger seats, a freight floor and extra fuel tanks in the cabin. After operating the type as intended, and with the war in North Africa concluded, BOAC transferred its Warwicks to Transport Command in early 1944.

A subsequent, more focused, military requirement for a Warwick transport for the RAF was issued to Vickers which developed the Warwick C.III. This variant incorporated glider towing gear and the usual ventral turret opening used as an exit for paratrooper deployment. The type was also fitted with a ventral pannier that incorporated four fuel tanks, rather than the cabin tanks of the C.I, which allowed the type to carry up to 30 troops. The Warwick C.III was rejected as a paratroop carrier by the

The Vickers Warwick was another bomber that had been overtaken by events and deemed unsuitable for Bomber Command. Like the other RAF variants, the Warwick C.III was powered by the Pratt & Whitney Double Wasp. This example, HG224, has had its pannier removed. (Blue Envoy Collection)

Airborne Forces Experimental Establishment at Beaulieu, which restricted it to a trooping role. The Warwick C.III entered service in June 1944, but, within two years, the type had been withdrawn from service, with only a handful used for research and development work.

The last of the converted bombers was a type that was something of an oddity in the inventory of British World War Two aircraft. Intended to use non-strategic materials, the Albemarle started life as the Bristol Type 155 before being transferred to Armstrong Whitworth, which designated it as the AW.41. The AW.41 used a steel and wood composite for its structure and was skinned with plywood, which enabled the airframe to be built by small factories that were unfamiliar with aircraft construction. The Albemarle was powered by a pair of Bristol Hercules XI, rated at 1,590hp (1,190kW), that gave it plenty of power for glider towing. In one nod to the future, the machine used a tricycle undercarriage at a time when British aircraft were still predominantly 'tail-draggers'.

The Albemarle had been designed as a bomber/reconnaissance aircraft to meet Specification 17/38, but due to production delays, it had, like the Warwick, been overtaken by events and was thus obsolete as a bomber by the time it was ready for service in mid-1942. As was now customary, the Albemarle was destined for the transport role and since it had not been specified to carry troops, was considered unsuitable for trooping duties. The Albemarle could carry ten paratroops but was assigned to glider towing duties and entered service as the Albemarle GT.1.

The type made its operational debut in July 1943 during Operation *Husky*, the invasion of Sicily, with 28 Albemarles towing Horsa gliders. The air assault aspect of *Husky* involved US and British airborne forces but was blighted by stronger-than-expected winds which scattered the gliders, with only 12 Horsas from the entire force reaching their objectives. The Albemarles subsequently took part in operations *Overlord*, *Market Garden* and *Varsity*, towing gliders rather than dropping parachutists. The Albemarle also served as a 'Special Transport' designated ST.1, II, V and VI, but as new transports became available, and the war ended, they were soon retired, with the last example leaving RAF service in February 1946.

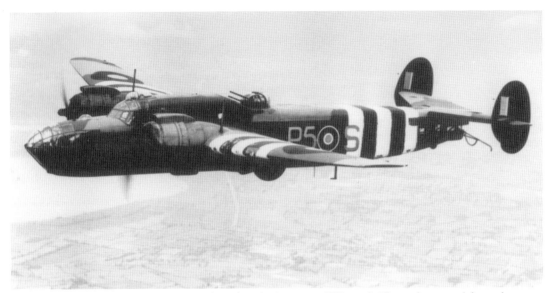

Obsolete as a bomber by the time it entered service, the Armstrong Whitworth Albemarle was mainly used as a glider tug. This Albemarle IV, V1823, of 297 Sqn, and resplendent on invasion stripes, towed Horsa gliders on operations *Tonga* and *Mallard*, the airborne assault aspects of *Overlord*. (Via Vic Flintham)

The Airspeed Horsa was the workhorse of British glider forces. Horsa II RZ155 was one of the last assault gliders in British service. The Horsa II had a hinged nose section and twin nosewheels. The hinged nose allowed large loads to be 'end loaded' into the cabin. (Via Vic Flintham)

Meanwhile in America, the Douglas Aircraft Company had modified its DC-3 airliner to produce a military transport for the US Army Air Corps. Douglas reinforced the floor, added fittings for a hoist system and fitted a large cargo door on the port side of the rear fuselage. This was designated as the C-47 ('C' being the US Army prefix for a transport, i.e. cargo aircraft) Skytrain and, by 1942, the first C-47s had been delivered under Lend-Lease to the RAF in India, with the RAF designating these as Dakota I.

The RAF acquired over 1,900 Dakotas, including a handful of the C-53 Skytroopers (as the Dakota II), a dedicated paratroop transport, and the Dakota formed the backbone of the RAF's transport fleet for the duration and beyond. The Dakota could carry up to 28 paratroopers, who jumped via a large door on the port side that allowed the 'stick' of troops to jump rapidly and with more kit than they could through the floor hatch of converted British bombers.

The large freight door of the Dakota I, III and IV allowed large items such as Jeeps to be loaded and unloaded, but for bulky items, the preferred method of delivery was the glider. British airborne forces used three types: the British Airspeed AS.51 Horsa and the US Waco CG-4 Hadrian for personnel and light vehicles such as Jeeps or 6-pounder (pdr) anti-tank guns, while heavier or bulky equipment such as the Tetrarch light tank or a 17-pdr anti-tank gun would be carried in the General Aircraft GAL.49 Hamilcar.

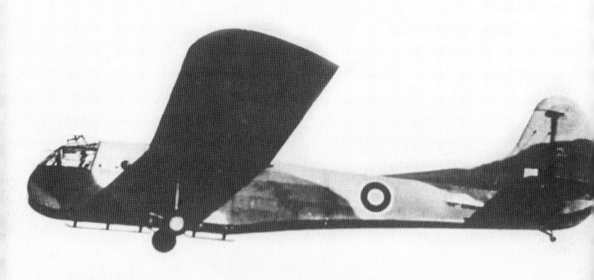

The US-built Waco Hadrian was widely used by British airborne forces in all theatres where glider assaults took place. The nose was hinged just aft of the cockpit and folded upwards to allow end-loading of equipment such as Jeeps. (Via Vic Flintham)

The Hamilcar was used to transport heavy and bulky equipment such as Universal Carriers, anti-tank guns or Tetrarch tanks. The Halifax was the preferred tug and with an eye to operations in the Far East, the Hamilcar X was fitted with a pair of Bristol Mercury engines, as seen on LA704. (Blue Envoy Collection)

The Horsa could carry up to 28 troops, but generally 20–25 was the normal load, with the pilots, members of the Glider Pilots Regiment, fighting alongside the glider-borne troops once on the ground. The Hadrian could carry 13 troops or a Jeep. A variety of types were used to tow the Horsa and Hadrian gliders, including Dakotas and Albemarles, with the Hamilcar towed by four-engined Handley Page Halifaxes.

As the Lancaster took on the brunt of the bomber offensive, Halifaxes were converted to transports and glider tugs, with the C.III particularly favoured for the latter task, specifically for towing Hamilcars. A number of Halifax bombers, B.II Specials, had been used to drop agents and weaponry into occupied Europe in support of the Special Operations Executive (SOE), particularly to resistance forces in distant countries such as Poland and Czechoslovakia. A classic example of such tasks was the delivery of Czech agents during Operation *Anthropoid*, the assassination of Reinhard Heydrich.

Dakota IIIs of 267 Sqn operated from Bari in southern Italy as part of the Balkans Air Force in support of partisans in Yugoslavia, Albania and Greece. The Dakotas ranged as far afield as Poland in support of resistance fighters and could not only deliver stores and personnel but evacuate wounded. (Via Vic Flintham)

This busy scene shows USAAF P-47s, P-51 (or possibly A-36), B-17s and B-24s sharing the airfield at Bari with RAF Douglas Dakota IIIs from 267 Sqn. These Dakotas were involved in dropping supplies to partisans in the Balkans from early 1943 but moved to the Burma theatre in February 1945. (Via Vic Flintham)

The Halifax was subsequently developed into specialised variants to support airborne forces and was equipped for delivering paratroopers and towing gliders. The first of these, the A.III, A.V and A.VII, were converted bombers, introduced pending the arrival of the dedicated Halifax A.IX. All could carry 12 parachutists, who exited via a floor hatch, while towing gear was fitted to allow the type to act as a tug for Horsa, Hamilcar and Hadrian gliders.

The first operational use of the Halifax as a glider tug was during Operation *Freshman* in November 1942, when two Horsas were towed to southern Norway carrying troops to attack the German heavy water plant at Vemork in the Norwegian district of Telemark. Both Horsas and one Halifax crashed. The operation was not a success but proved that operations with gliders were feasible and the heavy water plant was subsequently destroyed by Norwegian SOE agents. Airborne forces Halifaxes were subsequently used with great success in all British air assault operations after late 1942. The last Halifax variant in British military service was the A.IX, used by the Parachute Training School, which operated the type until 1949.

The Halifax also formed the basis of a military transport, the C.VIII, that would in turn become a civil transport aircraft after the war. The Halifax C.VIII was a B.VI stripped of its turrets, which were replaced with aerodynamic fairings and, as with the airborne forces' Halifaxes, the C.VIII could deliver paratroopers, again through a ventral hatch. A civil variant of the Halifax C.VIII was called the Halton and was fitted with a ventral pannier that could be installed in the bomb bay but extended below the fuselage line. The pannier could carry 8,000lb (3,636kg) of freight and, during the Berlin Airlift, a few of the panniers were replaced with large fuel tanks to carry diesel into West Berlin.

Another method to carry the parachute troops' support equipment, such as mortars and anti-tank weapons, was to use the CLE container. This was a cylindrical container, 5ft 7in (1.7m) long and

The Halifax A.III was the first of the airborne forces' support Halifaxes. These were configured for glider towing and paratrooper delivery. They could also carry a Jeep and 6-pdr anti-tank gun semi-recessed in the bomb bay. This Halifax has just released a Jeep. The pans under the wheels acted as shock absorbers. (Blue Envoy Collection)

1ft 4in (0.4m) in diameter, with a parachute at one end and an impact-absorbing section at the other. It was split along its length and hinged along one side to allow speedy access to the kit inside.

Known as the 'CLE', which stood for a variety of terms, such as Central Landing Establishment (who developed the container) and Container, Land Equipment, they were ultimately designated as Container, Light Equipment. The CLE's parachutes were colour coded to identify whether they carried weapons and ammunition (red), tools and stores (white), radios (green) or rations (blue). For air delivery, CLEs could be mounted in racks under the aircraft or inside the cabin, but to speed up the delivery of the troops, ventral carriage would be best. Post-war, RAF transport and support aircraft were fitted with racks to carry a number of CLEs, with the larger transports such as the Hastings and Beverley fitted with a stores aimer's position in the nose.

From late 1943, many Short Stirlings were converted to the transport role as the Stirling IV and V and used for paratrooping and glider towing. Like the Halifaxes, the Stirling IVs had their nose and dorsal turrets removed, while the Stirling V had all its turrets removed. Interestingly, in the vein of the bomber/transport requirements, the original specification B.12/36 for the Short Stirling stated that up to 24 troops could be carried. The Stirling V had a large freight door, hinged at the bottom, on the starboard side that could be used to load bulky cargo such as Jeeps. The Stirling V, in a portent to the future, also had an upward-opening nose, but the ground angle of the Stirling made both openings awkward to use, although a block and tackle was supplied for nose loading.

The Stirling IVs were first used to tow Horsa gliders for Operation *Overlord* and were subsequently used as tugs for *Market Garden* and *Varsity*. One other role for the Stirling IV was support for ground forces by dropping food and ammunition containers to airborne troops while the Second Tactical Air Force's forward airfields were supplied with fuel and stores by Stirlings.

Stirling Vs arrived in service during January 1945 and were mostly involved in trooping flights. By the end of the war in Europe, and with the focus moving to the war with Japan, Stirling Vs were conducting trooping flights to India. The Stirling Vs were soon replaced on these routes by the Avro York and the last Stirling in RAF service was retired at Bombay (now Mumbai) in July 1946.

The end of the war in Europe saw the focus of the nation's effort move to the Far East. As noted above, air supply had been key to many of the DUKE forces operations in the Burma theatre, with US-supplied Dakotas forming the backbone of these logistics support operations. Air drops of food

The Short Stirling C.IV and V were fitted with a freight door on the starboard rear fuselage. Seen here with a Jeep being loaded during trials, the door could act as a platform for manoeuvring vehicles or cargo into the aircraft. (Blue Envoy Collection)

and ammunition had been invaluable in the hard fighting to halt the Japanese *U-Go* offensive in northeast India between April and June 1944. United States Army Air Force (USAAF) and RAF transports, mainly Dakotas, delivered over 500 tons (508 tonnes) of stores to troops besieged at Kohima and Imphal. Supply of troops by air and evacuation of wounded by Dakotas and light aircraft, such as Austers and Sentinels, allowed DUKE forces to push the Japanese Army into retreat in India and Burma. Had the war continued, the Allied ground forces, with their operational momentum maintained by air transport and close air support, would have ultimately defeated Japanese forces in that theatre.

With the end of the war in the Far East, the British found themselves in a peculiar situation, particularly in Indo-China. Due to the rules of Lend-Lease, US-supplied equipment had to be paid for, returned or destroyed, which led to the withdrawal of many US types, including the Dakota, leading to a shortage of transport aircraft. As a result, Imperial Japanese Army Air Force aircraft, such as the Kawasaki Ki.48 'Lily' bomber and, ironically, the Nakajima L2D 'Tabby', which was a licence-built Douglas DC-3, were pressed into service. Another reason for pressing Japanese aircraft into service was they could run on the low-octane fuel available in theatre, rather than transporting higher-octane fuel from Allied stock.

Another Douglas product entered RAF service towards the end of the war when ten C-54Ds were transferred to the RAF, serving as the Skymaster I for a short period before being returned under Lend-Lease rules. A single C-54B was used by Winston Churchill as his personal transport after the loss of Consolidated Liberator II *Commando* in late March 1945.

The RAF ended the war with the bulk of its transport fleet comprising US types plus the converted bombers, but it intended to replace all of these in the long term, especially as the US types had been supplied under Lend-Lease and had to be either returned or destroyed. The RAF's wartime experiences would take a decade to be applied. Until the late 1950s, the RAF's transport aircraft would comprise types that were either derived from bombers and airliners or, as could be argued in the Hastings' case, a larger four-engined Dakota. By the end of the 1950s, a completely new generation of transports would be entering service, and these incorporated the many lessons from the war.

The second Douglas C-54 Skymaster to enter RAF service, KL977, shows its large cargo door in the rear fuselage and level stance, thanks to its tricycle undercarriage. The C-54s were returned to the US once the war was won. (Blue Envoy Collection)

Chapter 4

The Not-So-New Generation

Air supply, one of the most valuable applications of air power in the post-war era, finds its genesis more in South-East Asia than in any other theatre of the Second World War.

Air Commodore Henry Probert, *The Forgotten Air Force: The Royal Air Force in the War Against Japan 1941–1945*, Brassey, 1996

I n essence, nothing had really changed in British transport aircraft since the Great War – converted bombers and, aside from the Victoria/Vernon with increased diameter fuselages, the basic bomber, minus turrets and with doors added, was the norm. Avro at Manchester aimed to change that with their Type 685 York. Intended to meet Specification C.1/43 and OR.113, the York married the wings, engines, undercarriage and empennage from the Lancaster with a new square-section fuselage. Intended as a passenger aircraft, the York entered RAF service in early 1945 with later variants configured for freight only or mixed freight/passengers.

The new generation of transports that were specified in the last years of the war included the Vickers Valetta C1 such as VL280 and the Hastings, seen here with WJ338 in its C2 guise with a larger tailplane and more powerful engines. These replaced the huge number of Dakotas supplied under Lend-Lease that were either returned, sold or scrapped at the end of the war. (Blue Envoy Collection)

Winkle Brown's Strange Beast

Another, possibly unacknowledged at the time, influence on the development of transport aircraft was the Arado Ar 232B. For three years, the RAF's Air Intelligence Branch had puzzled over a German twin-engined aircraft that had first been observed at the Luftwaffe's Rechlin test centre. Designated *Rechlin 104*, the number referring to the type's wingspan in feet, it was noted in various locations covered by RAF photo-reconnaissance aircraft. A few months later, a four-engined version of the aircraft was captured on film at the Arado plant at Brandenburg, which became known as the *Brandenburg 110*. Intelligence from other sources as far apart as France and Norway allowed intelligence officers to produce a description of a very strange looking aircraft, but there were no clues to its name or designation. The *Brandenburg 110*'s true identity as the Arado Ar 232B was only clarified in the days following D-Day when German aircraft recognition posters were discovered in a bunker.

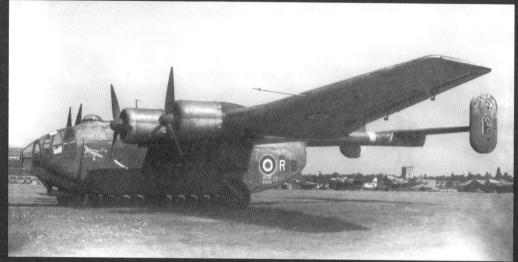

The Arado Ar 232B could be described as the original tactical transport. It possessed lots of power, a high-flotation undercarriage, end-loading at truck-bed height and blown flaps, all of which are found on modern transport aircraft. This example, Air Min 17/Werk Nummer 305002, was tested at RAE Farnborough in late 1945. (Via Phil Butler)

The Ar 232B had been designed for transport operations on the Eastern Front and bore all the hallmarks of all tactical transports: high wing, lots of power, high-flotation tricycle undercarriage, capacious hold with large rear doors for end-loading and a truck-bed level floor. It also had a flap blowing system for short field performance. The type impressed the British, who used it in support of the Farren Mission after VE Day to transport equipment to and from RAE Farnborough and, in correspondence with this author, Captain Eric 'Winkle' Brown described it as 'a strange beast with a sound functional purpose'.

Realistically, it was parallel evolution whereby problems were addressed in a similar fashion by different people. Contemporaneous with the Arado Ar 323B, the Budd RB-1 Conestoga of 1943 took a similar approach: high-wing, tricycle undercarriage, level cabin floor, end-loading rear ramp under a raised rear fuselage. Similarly, Miles Aircraft had developed its Aerovan, but this could only be described as a light transport, rather than a tactical transport for front-line use.

To replace the Dakotas that would need to be returned, a new generation of British transport aircraft was developed. Still based on bombers, such as the Avro York that was derived from the Lancaster, these had more practical fuselages more suited to the role. (Blue Envoy Collection)

Post-war, a new generation of transport aircraft appeared on the scene, but these, the Vickers Valetta (with a single 'l' unlike the capital of Malta) for Specification C.9/46 and the Handley Page Hastings to meet Specification C.3/44, were effectively modern, larger Dakotas that retained the tail dragger undercarriage and a large side door for cargo, neither of which were conducive to rapid loading or unloading; but two factors would impact the future development of transport aircraft.

The first factor that influenced development came from the British campaigns in the Far East. The DUKE forces involved in the Burma campaign became increasingly reliant upon air transport for delivery of materiel, and while parachutists were deployed, most operations involved air-landing of troops and kit, which required runways to be hacked out of the jungle. While the Dakota was capable of operating from such strips, they were far from ideal. The Hamilcar had shown that an airframe designed to carry bulky loads, such as bulldozers to build airstrips, was viable, so would form the basis of a cargo carrier for the war in the East. To operate the Hamilcar in the hot and high conditions of the Far East and to allow self-recovery, Specification X 4/44 was issued, which led to the Hamilcar X with a pair of 965hp (720kW) Bristol Mercury 31 engines. With the end of the war and gliders falling from favour in the post-war military world, the Hamilcar X was not required, although one example was converted into an airborne early warning test bed by the Telecommunications Research Establishment. Interestingly the Hamilcar, like the Horsa and Hadrian, did include a feature that is the mark of a modern military transport – end-loading.

Gliders pioneered end-loading, a feature that would become invaluable on military transport aircraft. The AS.58 Horsa II's fuselage was hinged to allow vehicles to be loaded and unloaded while the Hamilcar's nose swung open, as seen here, to allow a vehicle such as a Tetrarch tank to drive out. This example is a Hamilcar X, powered by a pair of Bristol Mercury engines to allow self-recovery. (Blue Envoy Collection)

A more practical machine was the Bristol Type 170 Freighter, which used a pair of Bristol Hercules engines, rated at 2,000hp (1,500kW), and featured a nose that opened to allow bulky loads such as vehicles to be driven in. Unfortunately for Bristol, despite being designed to meet Air Ministry Specification 22/44 and the later C.9/45 for a rugged transport aircraft, the RAF did not adopt it, preferring the Valetta. The Royal Canadian Air Force and Royal New Zealand Air Force operated the Type 170, but the only UK users were the Aircraft and Armament Experimental Establishment (A&AEE) and the Telecommunications Research Establishment. However, the answer to the RAF's tactical transport requirement has its origin, like all other tactical transports, in Germany's Arado Flugzeugwerke.

Although it was never operated by the RAF, the Bristol Type 170 Freighter was designed to meet an Air Ministry specification. This example was operated by the Royal Canadian Air Force and shows the large nose doors and ready access to the hold. (Terry Panopalis Collection)

The variety of British transport aircraft available in the immediate post-war era is summed up in this photograph of Heathrow Airport. Types include the Avro Tudor I, Bristol Freighter, Handley Page Halifax C.VIII, Avro XIX, Avro York and a Miles Messenger. (Blue Envoy Collection)

Three Avro York C.Is from 511 Sqn about to depart Luqa in Malta while enroute to the Far East. York MW123 is running up its engines and the chocks are away, ready for departure. Yorks maintained the trunk routes from the UK, with Malta being one of the many stopovers on the route to the east. (Blue Envoy Collection)

Post-war Years

The second was the Berlin Airlift of 1948–49, which was prompted by the Soviet Union closing all land access to West Berlin, the portion of that city under the authority of the UK, US and France. Berlin was 100 miles (160km) east of the Inner German Border surrounded by the territory of the German Democratic Republic. The only access to the city was by air, via three air corridors, and to keep the citizens of West Berlin alive, the Western Allies commenced Operation *Plainfare* (UK name), *Vittles* (US name) and *Pelican* (Australian name). The operation was a success and continued until May 1949 when the Soviets lifted the blockade, but it did show that the transport types in use at the time were unsuitable to the rapid loading/unloading required for an airlift on such a large scale. Ultimately, Major General William H. Tunner of the United States Air Force (USAF) took the decision to focus on using larger types with tricycle undercarriages, such as the Douglas C-54, as they were easier to load and unload thanks to their level floor.

Left: To increase the pace of deliveries, USAF Major General Tunner decreed that large aircraft with tricycle undercarriage, such as the Douglas C-54 Skymaster seen here, should be a priority for the Berlin Airlift, as they were quicker to load and unload. RAF types on the operation were mainly tail draggers.

Below: Handley Page converted the Halifax into a civil passenger/cargo aircraft called the Halton. This example is fitted with a large tank pannier to carry diesel fuel into West Berlin during the airlift. (Blue Envoy Collection)

When the Hastings was designed (its specification, C.3/44, was issued in 1944) the lessons from the war in the East and the innovations from Germany were yet to influence designers of transport aircraft. Handley Page produced a four-engined aircraft with a large cargo door on the port side of the rear fuselage, glider towing gear and loading beams under the wing centre section to carry large loads, such as a Jeep or a 6-pdr anti-tank gun, under the fuselage.

Handley Page's Hastings provided the RAF and the airborne operations with a large-capacity transport that could deliver men and materiel by parachute or airlanding. Hastings C1 TG507 was the tenth production example. TG507 had an interesting career, used as a VIP transport in the Far East, supported ELINT operations and ultimately converted to a MET3 for meteorological reconnaissance. (Blue Envoy Collection)

This unidentified Hastings is carrying a full complement of 20 CLE stores containers on the ventral stores racks. Also visible in this image is the glazing for the stores aimer's position in the nose. The Hastings could also carry vehicles such as Jeeps on ventral loading beams. (Blue Envoy Collection)

Compared with its converted bomber predecessors, the Vickers Valetta C.1 was, thanks to its large double doors, easier to load bulky items such as vehicles. The angled ramp also made vehicles quicker to load, as seen here with an aircraft tug. (Blue Envoy Collection)

The glider kit was soon removed as gliders disappeared from service, but as a troop transport the Hastings could carry 50 troops and was fitted with doors on the port and starboard sides of the rear fuselage for deployment of 35 paratroops, a role it fulfilled in campaigns such as Suez in November 1956. Dropping supplies to British forces wherever they operated was the Hastings' bread and butter. The Hastings remained in service for 30 years, ending its days as a radar trainer for the V-bombers, which in turn led to its use as a maritime radar reconnaissance aircraft during the Cod Wars of the 1970s!

Cargo handling could be an awkward process in a taildragger such as a Dakota, Hasting, or, in this instance, a Valetta C1. Loading an aircraft with a tricycle undercarriage was much easier thanks to the level cabin floor. If the aircraft featured end-loading at truck-bed height, even better. (Blue Envoy Collection)

The air loadmaster stands in the open parachute door of Vickers Valetta C1 VL263. Finished in bare metal, VL263 may be undergoing trials, as it was one of the earliest Valettas delivered to the RAF, arriving in February 1948. (Blue Envoy Collection)

The second post-war transport was a military transport variant of the Vickers Viking airliner, itself derived from the Wellington. The Valetta was developed to meet Specification C.9/46 as a multi-role transport that could be converted between roles such as trooping (with up to 34 troops), air ambulance, freight carrier or paratrooping with 20 parachutists. The Valetta took part in air assaults during the Suez campaign of 1956 and supported troops in Aden and Malaya throughout the 1950s and 1960s. The Valetta C2 was to meet Specification C.18/48 for a passenger variant configured to carry VIPs.

Comparison with the Valetta's contemporary in the US shows the difference in the two nations' approaches to tactical transport aircraft. US designs, such as the Fairchild C-82 Packet, C-123 Provider and the later C-119 Flying Boxcar, provided the Americans with very practical tactical transports with end-loading and tricycle undercarriages. In fairness, both the Valetta and Hastings were designed at a time when vertical envelopment by massed paratroop operations was the standard procedure for offensive operations into enemy territory.

Right: Valettas worked hard in support of British forces wherever they served. Valetta C1 VW182 is delivering stores to troops in the jungle of Malaya during Operation *Firedog*. Army operations in the rainforest were heavily dependent on resupply from the air. (Blue Envoy Collection)

Below: While the RAF was adopting the Valetta as a Dakota replacement, the USAF introduced types such as the Fairchild C-119 Flying Boxcar with tricycle undercarriage and end-loading. The C-119 entered service in 1949, replacing the C-47 and C-46. (Blue Envoy Collection)

Brough's Big 'Un

One reason the Bristol 170 probably failed to elicit an order from the RAF was that Transport Command had its eye on a large transport being developed by General Aircraft Ltd (GAL), developers of the Hamilcar. The Ar 232B provided the blueprint for post-war tactical transports.

General Aircraft Ltd's GAL.60 Universal Freighter was designed as a civil cargo aircraft, but after the company merged with Blackburn Aircraft, it was modified to produce the Beverley. Universal Freighter Mk.1 WF320 is seen flying over Beverley Minster. (Blue Envoy Collection).

In the immediate post-war period, there was also a British requirement for a Horsa glider replacement, X.30/46, for which GAL proposed the GAL.62, which incorporated features seen in the Ar 232B. The RAF was also interested in a large tactical transport to meet Specification C.3/46, and since gliders had faded into history by the late 1940s, GAL combined features of the GAL.62 with the GAL.60 and drew up the GAL.65 Universal Freighter Mk.2 with Centaurus, rather than Hercules, engines and with the merger of GAL and Blackburn Aircraft, the GAL.65 became the Blackburn B-101 – better known as the Beverley.

The Beverley C1 entered service in March 1956 and soon proved its worth, operating from austere airstrips, carrying loads within its capacious 10ft x 10ft x 40ft (3.05m x 3.05m x 12.19m) cabin up to a maximum of 45,000lb (20,408kg). For airdropping kit, up to 25,000lb (11,338kg) in a single drop, the clamshell doors had to be removed, as they could not be opened in flight. Up to 70 paratroops could be carried, with 30 of these in the aircraft's tail boom, and in a return to the days of the Whitley, they exited through a floor hatch, albeit a bespoke item, much larger than those on converted bombers such as the Whitley.

One important aspect of the Beverley, which would have repercussions in the future, was instruction given to the British Army by the Air Staff stating that if a piece of army kit did not fit into the Beverley's hold, it would not be dismantled and would not be carried by air. Another development, introduced as the Beverley was being developed, was the use of standardised cargo platforms.

The Blackburn Beverley's capacious hold could carry most vehicles, but whether this Leyland Hippo pressure refueller is being loaded or filling up the Beverley is not clear, but it does seem to be lined up for loading. For airdrops, the Beverley's hold doors had to be removed, as they could not be opened in flight. (Blue Envoy Collection)

Rugged, like the landscape. They may have been slow, and the engines may have leaked oil, but for operations in theatres such as Aden, the Beverley was perfect. Beverley XM103 operated with 84 Sqn from RAF Khormaksar. The squadron swapped its Beverleys for Andovers in 1968. (Blue Envoy Collection)

The slab-sided Blackburn Beverley is an imposing sight, around 30ft (9.1m) to the top of the fuselage, which is around twice the height of a double decker bus. Replacing the Beverley led to the procurement of the Hercules, but that was only after the AW.681 had been cancelled. (Terry Panopalis Collection)

These Medium and Heavy Stressed Platforms (MSP and HSP) first appeared in 1953. The MSP was an alloy frame, 3in (7.6cm) deep, 16ft (4.9m) long and 7ft (2.1m) wide, capable of supporting an 18,000lb (8,163kg) load, although a typical load would be a Land Rover and trailer or a field gun and ammunition. For heavier loads, such as armoured vehicles or construction plant, the HSP was used. This was 24ft 9in (7.5m) long and 8ft 7in (2.6m) and could carry a load weighing up to 35,000lb (15,873kg). The HSP required two 66ft-diameter (20.1m) extractor chutes to pull it from the aircraft hold, with the extractor chutes themselves deployed by a smaller, single 21ft-diameter (6.4m) drogue chute. Up to six of the 66ft (20.1m) parachutes would lower the load to the ground.

To assist take-off when loaded with heavy equipment, the Beverley could be fitted with Rocket-assisted Take-off Gear (RATOG) comprising ten Armstrong Siddeley Scarab solid rocket motors. These had originally developed for the Vickers Valiant V-bomber, but racks were designed for the Beverley to support up to five rockets each side of the fuselage.

The 49 Beverleys worked hard during their 12 years in service, especially 'East of Suez' in support of British forces in the deserts of Aden and rainforests of Borneo, soldiering on until they were retired in late 1967 with the arrival of the C-130K Hercules C1 or, in the case of 84 Sqn, the Hawker Siddeley Andover C1. Despite its looks, the Beverley incorporated all the lessons from the Arado Ar 232B and the Berlin Airlift – good take-off and landing performance from rough strips combined with parachute delivery of large items and end-loading from trucks.

As mentioned above, the Hastings was designed and accepted into service almost immediately after the war ended as the American-supplied transports were being returned or scrapped. A replacement for the Hastings was sought under Operational Requirement OR.323. Several proposals were put forward by the aircraft companies but, as ever, the Air Staff was looking to save money and the numerous proposals were dismissed on cost grounds.

To improve the Beverley's take-off performance at high all-up weights, rocket-assisted take-off (RATO) was tested. This comprised five Armstrong Siddeley Scarab rocket motors mounted on racks each side of the fuselage. The Beverley could clear a 50ft (15.2m) obstacle from a standing start in 800 yards (731m). (Blue Envoy Collection)

For dropping heavy or awkwardly shaped cargo, Medium and Heavy Stressed Platforms were developed. These allowed any load to be handled in the same way once it was attached to the platform. Here, a load on a Medium Stressed Platform has just left a Beverley hold, having been dragged by the drogue chute. (Blue Envoy Collection)

Meanwhile, at Bagington in Warwickshire, Armstrong Whitworth Aircraft (AWA) was developing a new civil cargo aircraft based on the AW.66, the aircraft the company had put forward for OR.323. This was a twin-Centaurus machine. However, for the civil market, Armstrong Whitworth changed the design to use four Rolls-Royce Dart turboprops rather than the two piston engines.

This became the AW650, a private venture by Armstrong Whitworth who were intent on developing a cargo aircraft for airlines such as British European Airways (BEA). The AW.650 was to be a twin-boom design with a fuselage pod with access to the main hold via the entire nose and rear of the pod opening to allow end-loading. The AW.650 was powered by four Rolls-Royce Dart turboprops, rated at 2,470shp (1,840kW), with one engine nacelle forming the forward portion of the tail booms, which also held the main undercarriage. The Ministry of Supply and the Air Staff were watching with interest, and eventually, when the AW.650 was compared with OR.323, the Air Staff decided that the AW.650 could, if modified, more or less meet the requirement. To cater for the differences, a new requirement, OR.344, and Specification C.195 were drawn up and issued to AWA to cover development of what became the AW.660 Argosy.

The RAF had no need for the swing nose, which was deleted, and a reinforced floor with 'Rolomat' was fitted. Rolomat was a freight handling system that comprised a series of rollers that allowed loads to be moved around the hold with comparative ease, and tie-down points to allow loads to be secured. The most significant change to the AW.650 was the redesign of the rear door to produce a horizontally split wedge that could be opened in flight or, when on the ground, the lower section served as a ramp

Right: The air loadmaster's view aft as a pair of Argosies form up for a photoshoot. One of the Argosy's claims to fame is that it was the first turboprop-powered aircraft to enter service with the RAF. (Blue Envoy Collection)

Below: Until 1971, a spick and span Argosy such as XR142 from 114 Sqn was used to support the RAF Red Arrows aerobatic team. The team's Folland Gnat T1s are lined up alongside XR142. (Terry Panopalis Collection)

to allow vehicles to be driven in. The twin-boom configuration allowed vehicles to be reversed up the ramp and, when lowered to horizontal, brought the ramp to truck bed height. With the rear doors open, loads of up to 14,000lb (6,350kg) could be paradropped if mounted on an MSP, a technique that allowed loads such as vehicles to be packaged for delivery by parachute. For the air assault mission, up to 54 paratroops could be carried, exiting through doors on each side of the rear fuselage.

The Argosy prototype G-APRL poses with a FV.601 Saladin armoured car and FV.603 Saracen armoured personnel carrier. These could be driven into the hold, although the Saracen might need its turret removed. In a tactical situation, if vehicles were to be deployed by air, the vehicles would be reversed in. (Blue Envoy Collection)

A sequence showing a Ferret armoured car being delivered by Argosy C1 XN817 during trials at the A&AEE. The top left photo shows the drogue chute that drags the Ferret from the aircraft. Top right shows the Ferret exiting the aircraft. Bottom left shows the Ferret on a Medium Stressed Platform and the parachute pack on the rear of the Ferret. Bottom right shows the four parachutes deployed. (Blue Envoy Collection)

One of the oddest episodes in the evolution of the Argosy was the Ministry of Supply's (MoS) intention to use the wing from the Shackleton maritime patrol aircraft for the AW.660, to save a bit of money, as it was ideally sized and took four engines. Unfortunately, the Shackleton wing was much heavier, used old construction techniques and the engine locations were deemed unsuitable for the AW.660. Sense prevailed and AWA's wing design was adopted, with a comparative weight saving of 400lb (181kg).

A particularly modern innovation proposed for the Argosy that did not make the production variant was the Autoland system with 'windscreen presentation' using a 'collimated flight director', well known today as a head-up display (HUD). Some at the Air Staff and Air Ministry considered Autoland and its HUD unnecessary, and as one member of the Air Staff stated, 'Is this an extravagance i.e. aren't we cluttering the flight deck?' HUDs for transport aircraft finally entered service in the 1990s on the McDonnell Douglas C-17A Globemaster III and Lockheed C-130J Hercules.

Above: The Armstrong Whitworth Argosy was a familiar sight 'East of Suez', supporting British forces even as they withdrew. Argosy C1s XP411, XP412 and XP437 from 105 Sqn Middle East Air Force, RAF Khormaksar, fly past the Crater, Aden. Argosy XP411 is preserved at the RAF Museum Cosford. (Blue Envoy Collection)

Right: Originally designed as AW.650 Argosy civil cargo aircraft, Armstrong Whitworth took the AW.650, deleted the hinged nose and tail doors and modified the rear fuselage with horizontally split doors that opened in flight to allow air delivery of stores. The result was the AW.660 Argosy C1. While the official nickname was 'Whistling Wheelbarrow' most knew it as the 'Whistling Tit' for reasons obvious in the photo. (Terry Panopalis Collection)

The Argosy was not without its critics, with one pointing out that the cabin cross-section was nowhere near the 10ft x 10ft (3.05m x 3.05m) laid out in OR.323, but that had been addressed in OR.344, which had been pretty much written around the AW.650. The redesigned machine became the AW.660 Argosy C1 and entered service with 105 Sqn in March 1962, replacing Hastings transports. The Argosy's distinctive whistling sound was heard around the world, with Argosies operating in support of Britain's forces as the 'Withdrawal from Empire' gained momentum. From 1970, it was replaced by the C-130K but soldiered on in the transport role until 1975. Nine examples were retained in the radar calibration and training roles until 1978, but it was as a civil cargo aircraft in New Zealand and Alaska that the Argosy ended its days. The AWA design had gone full circle.

Left: A Transport Command Argosy C1 shares a tropical ramp with an Air Madagascar Boeing 707 and a Coastal Command Shackleton MR2 (just visible to the left). The main rear ramp is open and the secondary ramps visible, but only one is deployed. The 'elephant's foot' used to prevent the aircraft tipping backwards can be seen under the starboard ramp. (Terry Panopalis Collection)

Below: From the Belfast to the Basset: RAF Abingdon, 1968. The RAF's transport fleet – Air Support Command – was at its zenith in 1968, and this display would never be seen again. Interestingly, three types in this 1968 photo, C-130, VC10 and HS.125, were still in service 40 years later. (Blue Envoy Collection)

Chapter 5

Beyond the Barrier

All okay, steaming slowly south easterly, no sign of scurvy on board.
Unidentified Belfast aircrew updating air traffic control
after missing a radio check

To fill the requirement for a strategic transport to carry kit to the Mounting Bases, the Air Staff, in 1959, drew up Air Staff Requirement ASR.371/Specification C.203. Handley Page submitted the HP.111, a jet transport based on the Victor's wings and empennage, while Hawker, Avro and Short submitted aircraft powered by turboprops. The Hawker P.1131 featured nose and tail end-loading, the Avro Type 743 had rear cargo doors, while the Short Britannic 1 used Bristol Britannia wings and tail on a large-diameter fuselage. The Hawker and Avro designs were dismissed at an early stage, leaving the Handley Page and Short designs.

Seen flying over the mangrove swamps in northeast Singapore, Belfast XR366 has yet to be fitted with the drag reduction strakes under the tailplanes. It does have the damping strakes added to improve handling and reduce a tendency to Dutch roll. Unfortunately, fixing that increased drag, thus further reducing speed! (Blue Envoy Collection)

A Policy for the 1960s

The wars that the United Kingdom had fought in the 15 years since the end of World War Two had been counter-insurgency operations that involved the RAF operating in support of the Army. By the end of the 1950s, there was no doubt that, no matter how hard the British fought, the colonies would become independent. Within the British government, there was a view that British forces might be required to fight in these newly independent countries to protect British interests. From this arose the 'Mounting Base Strategy' whereby stores and equipment were stockpiled in locations around the Indian Ocean such as Gan, Singapore and Labuan. If a situation arose where intervention was required, troops and support personnel would be flown in on strategic transports prior to launching air assault operations using tactical transports and helicopters.

Three transport types would be key to the Mounting Base Strategy: a strategic airlifter, a strategic trooper and a tactical airlifter. As ever, despite issuing requirements and specifications, none of these went as the Air Staff planned. The strategic airlifter was the Short Belfast rather than Handley Page's HP.111, and after much procrastination the Vickers VC10 filled the strategic trooper role, which left the tactical transport, leading to the Armstrong Whitworth AW.681, a complex STOL transport.

The Mounting Base Strategy was short-lived, as the 'Withdrawal from Empire' happened at a faster pace than originally planned and by the mid-1960s, intervention in newly independent countries was unattractive to the British government. By 1971, the British presence East of Suez had all but gone.

'See ya!' Two locals wave goodbye to the crew of Belfast XR369 *Spartacus* as it prepares to leave Gan for the last time. If anything sums up British policy in the late 1960s, it is this photo. Gan was to be a Mounting Base and the Belfast was developed to support these. Both were deemed unnecessary by 1965. (Blue Envoy Collection)

Above left: **The Air Staff wanted a modern jet aircraft to meet its strategic transport needs. Handley Page's HP.111 was the Air Staff's choice, but the Short Belfast was procured. This Handley Page artwork shows how the HP.111 combined Victor-derived wings and tail with a capacious fuselage. (Blue Envoy Collection)**

Above right: **When the Belfast was specified, its main task was to move expensive and complex kit to the Mounting Bases. This Belfast is being loaded with Westland Wessex HC2 XR524. As can be seen, the helicopter has been stripped of anything that stuck out! Modern helicopters are designed for carriage in transport aircraft. (Blue Envoy Collection)**

Despite the Air Staff's preference for the HP.111, the Britannic 3A (with a new wing design and other modifications) was selected for production as the Short SC.5/10. The Air Staff wanted an all-jet fleet, and it was pointed out in a debate in the House of Lords that any aircraft with propellers would look anachronistic by the 1970s.

The name Britannic was dropped in early 1959, as it could be confused with the Britannia in communications, with the name Belfast selected instead. An order for ten production aircraft was placed in early 1960 and the first example, XR362, took to the air at Short's Sydenham airfield on 5 January 1964. Flight trials soon revealed that the Belfast, never expected to be quick, suffered from suction drag on the rear fuselage, a phenomenon that reduced the Belfast's speed and, as a result, its payload/range fell by 10 per cent, prompting the nickname 'Belslow'. Work by Short and the Royal Aircraft Establishment (RAE) produced a fix for the problem in the form a pair of strakes on the rear fuselage below the tailplanes alongside the cargo ramp that reduced the amount of suction drag. Another problem solved by strakes was the Belfast's propensity to 'Dutch roll', which was solved by strakes along the length of the cargo ramp. The lessons learned from the Belfast were subsequently applied to later transports, which now feature a longer rear fuselage. Despite the modifications, the Belfast was still slower than the RAF desired, so the nickname stuck.

The first Belfast, XR367, entered service with 53 Sqn in January 1966 and all ten production examples had been delivered by June 1967, all serving with 53 Sqn. The Belfast's capacious hold could accommodate bulky and heavy loads such as the FV431 Abbot self-propelled gun and large, but not especially heavy, loads such as Wessex helicopters with their rotors removed. The Belfasts plied their

Above left: This unidentified Belfast has been modified with the drag reduction strakes below the tailplanes. Not visible in this view are the damping strakes on the cargo ramp. The Belfast was intended to carry expensive or high-technology kit that could not be stockpiled. In this case, it is a FV.433 Abbot 105mm self-propelled gun. (Blue Envoy Collection)

Above right: Belfast XR363, *Goliath*, about to be loaded with a FV.701 Ferret, a FV.433 Abbot and a FV.601 Saladin at Brize Norton. These vehicles represented a load of 70,340lb (31,900kg). Short liked to show how much kit could be carried by a Belfast, even claiming it could carry a FV.4201 Chieftain main battle tank. Also of note is that *Goliath* has yet to be fitted with drag reduction strakes. (Blue Envoy Collection)

trade around the world, but no sooner had they arrived in service in 1967, they became involved in returning British kit from overseas – which was the opposite of their original requirement.

By 1975, the 'Withdrawal from Empire' was almost complete, and the aircraft types acquired to support East of Suez were deemed superfluous to requirements, so the Belfasts were to be disposed of. By mid-1976, 53 Sqn was disbanded and its Belfasts stored at RAF Kemble awaiting disposal, although

Short Belfast C1 XR366 *Atlas* of 53 Sqn being loaded with Westland Wessex HC2s of 72 Sqn. The Belfast could carry two Westland Wessex aircraft, but both had to be specially prepared and loaded on a carrying frame, as seen here. The latest generation of helicopters can be prepared for airlift in hours rather than days. (Blue Envoy Collection)

one example, XR371 *Enceladus*, was delivered to the RAF Museum at Cosford, where it remains on display to this day. Of the other nine Belfasts, four were bought by Rolls-Royce for their Tyne engines before being scrapped, while the remaining five were bought by Transmeridian Air Cargo (TAC) HeavyLift for the civil cargo market. Belfast XR362 *Samson* was used for certification, while XR365 *Hector* and XR368 *Theseus* were operated in the outsized cargo role from 1980, with the other two used for spares. Stripped of military kit, the civil Belfast could carry a greater payload than during their RAF careers and carried outsized loads that could not fit inside the Boeing 747F. In a supreme irony, these Belfasts were chartered by the RAF to support operations in the South Atlantic in 1982 for Operation *Corporate* and to Saudi Arabia during Operation *Granby* in 1991. In each case, the Belfast carried equipment that was too large for the RAF's Hercules, but what this really did was highlight the RAF's need for such a capability. That would be addressed in the 21st century.

Right: A rare look at the upper surfaces of a Belfast C1, in this case XR362 *Samson*, complete with Air Support Command titles. The inflight refuelling probe above the cockpit and the length of its ducting along the forward fuselage can be seen. Not visible in this photo are the two drag reduction strakes under the tailplanes. (Blue Envoy Collection)

Below: Paid off by the RAF in the mid-1970s, the Short Belfast fleet gained a new lease of life in the following two decades. Within six years of leaving service, the Ministry of Defence was chartering Belfasts, such as G-BEPS, on a regular basis to support operations around the world. (Blue Envoy Collection)

Chapter 6

Close Support

You will recall the nonsense we had over the galley not being able to accept RAF-type plates, and the requirement to change it – at great cost. You very rightly gave this short shrift.

Air Chief Marshal Sir Edmund Hudlestone, Air Officer Commanding-in-Chief
Transport Command, in defence of the Military Herald, 25 October 1962

O
ne role for fixed-wing aircraft no longer exists in Western air forces: light tactical transport. Superseded by helicopters, few air forces operate such aircraft and their demise reflected the rise of the tactical support helicopter, which in turn was made possible by the gas turbine.

In the early days of military flying, any type of aircraft that could carry a payload, such as the BE.2c or DH.4, found itself pressed into service as a transport aircraft. By the end of World War Two, the troops in the field were being supported by supplies dropped (literally in some cases) from aircraft or flown in on gliders. In the jungles of the Far East, airstrips capable of handling a light aircraft such as an Auster were hacked out of the bush, while in some cases, such as Chindit operations, strips large enough to handle Dakotas were built.

The majority of Pioneer CC1s were operated East of Suez, and Pioneer CC1 XJ465 of 209 Sqn was based at RAF Seletar in Singapore. Although some were camouflaged, most Pioneers, such as XJ465, were natural metal with Day-Glo patches. These Pioneers appear to be on a dispersed site, as the 'ramp' is covered with Prefabricated Surfacing, Airfield (PSA). (Blue Envoy Collection)

Pioneering

Based on the experience of operating liaison aircraft in the jungles of Burma, the Air Ministry drew up Specification A.4/45, Air Staff Requirement OR.164, for a light liaison and casualty evacuation (casevac) aircraft that could operate from short strips.

Scottish Aviation Ltd (SAL) won the tender process and built the Scottish Aviation Pioneer I, also known as the Prestwick Pioneer. Originally powered by a 240hp (179kW) de Havilland Gipsy Queen straight-six, this was soon replaced with a 520hp (388kW) Alvis Leonides radial engine. This more powerful version, which SAL called the Pioneer II, was ordered by the RAF and entered service in August 1953 as the Pioneer CC1 (CC signifying 'communications' and 'cargo').

The Pioneer's STOL performance was phenomenal, with a take-off run of 75 yards (68.6m) and landing in 67 yards (61.3m), thanks to large Fowler flaps and full-span leading-edge slats. These numbers probably relate to light weights and ideal conditions, but not withstanding some marketing hyperbolae, the Pioneer's performance was impressive.

Forty Pioneers were procured, and most served East of Suez, becoming highly valued as a casevac machine in climates as diverse as Aden, Borneo, Malaya and Cyprus. They were used to supply army outposts and only required a strip 150 yards (68.7m) long and 20 yards (18.3m) wide! Given the nature of the flying conducted by the Pioneer squadrons, it will come as no surprise that 230 Sqn was re-equipped with Westland Whirlwind HAR10 helicopters in June 1962.

Like the RAF, the Malaysian Air Force operated the Pioneer and Twin Pioneer. The larger size of the Twin Pioneer is not readily apparent in this image, but its wingspan was 26ft 9in (8.15m) greater than its sibling. Both could operate from similar-sized airstrips. (Blue Envoy Collection)

The Pioneer CC1 fleet suffered considerable attrition, which, given the type's usual haunts, is understandable and, by late 1969, more than half of the fleet had been written off and the Pioneers were being withdrawn from service. The Pioneer was another type made redundant by the rapidly improving performance of helicopters such as the Whirlwind HAR10 and the Wessex HC2, while the Army itself was acquiring Westland Scout AH1s for the Army Air Corps. The last Pioneer CC1 was retired from RAF service in February 1970, but the type continued in service with the Royal Malaysian Air Force and Royal Ceylon Air Force.

Hot on the heels of the Pioneer CC1, SAL developed the Twin Pioneer, a larger machine with two Leonides engines that could carry a payload of up to 3,400lb (1,542kg) into strips not much larger than those used by the Pioneer CC1. Like its single-engined predecessor, the Twin Pioneer had full-span leading-edge slats and large Fowler flaps and, thus equipped, possessed superb STOL performance. The Twin Pioneer was selected to meet the Air Ministry's Specification C.186, and the first Twin Pioneer CC1 took to the air in August 1957, with first deliveries to 76 Sqn at Khormaksar in early 1958.

Left: While the USAF has its 'Elephant Walks' of KC-135 tankers, the RAF had 'Pioneer Parades' on a much-reduced scale. Four Twin Pioneers taxi out to take off from a newly finished airfield somewhere in the Far East. (Blue Envoy Collection)

Below: The Twin Pioneer CC2 featured Pratt & Whitney Wasp R-1340 engines rather than Alvis Leonides, with most of the surviving CC1s upgraded to CC2s. This CC2, XM961, seen in 1965, is in a European colour scheme while operated by 230 Sqn at RAF Benson. It was later sold to the civil market and is preserved at the National Museum of Flight at East Fortune. (Terry Panopalis Collection)

The Twin Pioneer carried personnel and equipment, and conducted casevac, light freighting, supply dropping, paratrooping and medium-level bombing operations in the British dependencies and protectorates. For the bombing role the Twin Pioneer could carry a bombload of up to 2,000lb (907kg) on pylons fitted to hardpoints on the stub wings that attached the undercarriage struts to the fuselage. These could also carry the CLE containers used by paratroops for their heavy weapons and other kit. Trials were also conducted with the Nord SS.11 anti-tank missile, with a pair carried on pylons under each outer wing.

SAL delivered the first of 32 Twin Pioneer CC1s in 1956 and these mainly operated East of Suez, providing sterling service during the Malayan Emergency and Indonesian Confrontation. A further seven examples of the CC2, essentially a civil version with Pratt & Whitney Wasp R-1340 engines, were delivered to the RAF. The surviving Twin Pioneer CC1 fleet was re-engined to bring them up to CC2 standard.

The Twin Pioneers also operated in Aden from 1958, supplementing the Pioneer CC1s that operated from Khormaksar. The Twin Pioneer was finally withdrawn in 1968, replaced by the Andover, although that type lacked the true STOL capability of the Twin Pioneer. A single Twin Pioneer CC2 survived until 1974, operated by the Empire Test Pilots' School for STOL training.

The Air Staff did not, in the immediate post-war period, issue a requirement for what would become known as a light tactical transport, but used Valettas, once most of the Dakotas had been retired, to support troops in the field. However, by having more than a passing interest in the support of its troops, it was the British Army General Staff in the War Office that outlined its needs for air support. The General Staff in 1958 produced a document titled *Army Requirements in the Middle Range of Aircraft*, which outlined the tasks required for tactical transport aircraft in a limited war. The Air Council examined the Army's document and in late February 1959 produced *Army Requirements for Short-Range Transport Aircraft*, advising that Bristol Belvederes, Westland Whirlwinds and Westminsters, plus the SAL Twin Pioneer, could meet the Army's needs.

Meanwhile, at the Air Ministry, there was a growing realisation that the Valettas were getting long in the tooth and therefore a requirement for a replacement was drawn up. A year after it expressed its views on a support type, the General Staff revised its needs and how to meet them – the Fairey

The light tactical transport and its nemesis. SAL Twin Pioneer CC1 XL993 (which is fitted with launch rails for the Nord SS.11 missile) and a Bristol Belvedere. The roles of the Twin Pioneer and Andover were ultimately replaced by helicopters such as the Puma and Chinook. (Blue Envoy Collection)

Handley Page's proposal for the Light Cargo Aircraft was the HP.124 based on the Herald airliner. Politics intervened, and the Air Staff received the Avro 748MF rather than the preferred HP.124. (Blue Envoy Collection)

Rotodyne Z, a larger version of the prototype Rotodyne would be ideal. Unfortunately, the Rotodyne was pricey to buy and operate, and late, so might not have been available when needed.

Attention turned to acquiring an existing fixed-wing design, called the 'Light Cargo Aircraft'. Three types seemed feasible: the Handley Page HP.124 Military Herald, the Avro 758 (a high-wing variant of the Avro 748) and the de Havilland Canada Caribou. All three featured end-loading and could carry an MSP for airdropping vehicles and equipment. The Light Cargo Aircraft was intended to support operations launched from the Mounting Bases and be capable of operating in and out of forward strips, many built by the intervention force.

The Avro 758 was too heavy, so Avro proposed the 748MF (Military Freighter), a standard Avro 748 with a new upswept rear fuselage to allow end-loading, plus a 'kneeling' main undercarriage to bring the ramp to truck bed height. On the other hand, the Air Staff favoured the Military Herald, but politics intervened, and since Handley Page refused to be merged with other aircraft companies, its design was dropped in favour of the Avro 748MF. The ministries were determined not to buy the Handley Page machine, and at one stage the argument against the Military Herald hinged on the size of the galley and the size of plates! In April 1963, Operational Requirement OR.370 and Specification C.327 were issued to Hawker Siddeley at Woodford.

The Avro 748 was soon renamed under the Hawker Siddeley designation system as the HS.748, while the 748MF included sufficient changes from the original airframe to merit a new designation as the HS.780. HS.748 G-ARRV was modified to become the prototype HS.780. These changes included uprated Rolls-Royce Dart RDa.12 turboprops driving larger propellers, which in turn required the engine mountings to be moved slightly outboard. A new upswept rear fuselage with dihedral tailplanes also incorporated horizontally split doors, with the upper sections opening upwards and outwards, while the lower section opened downwards to form a loading ramp. To bring that ramp closer to the ground or level with a truck bed, the main undercarriage 'knelt', and the nose oleo extended to lower the rear of the aircraft. This was another feature pioneered on the Arado Ar 232 but has since featured on the Lockheed C-5 Galaxy and C-160 Transall, albeit the nose wheel on the Galaxy. On the flip side of a kneeling undercarriage in relation to transport aircraft, the Boeing AH-64 Apache's main gear 'kneels' to ease loading into transport aircraft such as the Galaxy and Globemaster.

Somewhat confusingly, six 'standard' HS.748s were acquired to meet Specification C.219/ASR.373 and designated as the Andover CC2 and mainly used for VIP work with 32 Sqn. Two of these Andover CC2s, XS789 and XS790, were allocated to The Queen's Flight and served until replaced with the BAe 146 in 1986.

The first HS.780, called the Andover C1 in RAF service, was delivered in 1966 and three squadrons would operate it: 46 Sqn at Abingdon, 52 Sqn at Seletar in Singapore and 84 Sqn at Sharjah in the Trucial States (now the United Arab Emirates). The Andover's service East of Suez would prove to be its undoing, and in less than a decade the Andovers had gone. Like the Belfast and Britannia, they were no longer required for their intended role, which in the Andover's case would now be met by large helicopters such as the Chinook. The Andover could carry a payload of 14,300lb (6,485kg) payload, which is approximately 10,000lb (4,535kg) *less* than a Chinook, which can deliver that payload (including underslung vehicles that could not have fitted inside an Andover) without the need for an airstrip. As a result, the Andover, and most tactical transports in its class, has been blown away by the Chinook.

Right: Avro converted 748 G-ARRV to become the 748MF, which soon became the prototype for the HS780 Andover. This view of G-ARRV shows the rear fuselage modifications including dihedral tailplanes with tail ramp and rear doors open for delivery of stores. The image shows that end-loading was possible but required a kneeling undercarriage. (Blue Envoy Collection).

Below: To bring the Andover's tail ramp to truck-bed height, or to allow vehicles to drive in, the type was fitted with a kneeling main undercarriage. The difference in ground stance can be seen in this photo of a pair of 46 Sqn Andovers with aircraft on the right 'kneeling'. (Blue Envoy Collection)

RAF Andovers were delivered in the mid-stone and sand, with black undersides, colour scheme used on most transports operating East of Suez. The white area above the cockpit reflects heat and keeps the cockpit cool. At least that was the intention. Andover C1 XS602 of 46 Sqn is on the approach to Abingdon in 1966. (Terry Panopalis Collection)

One interesting postscript to the Andover's service was its use as a reconnaissance aircraft, covert and overt. The Pembrokes of 60 Sqn had been conducting clandestine photographic reconnaissance flights along the Berlin air corridors, but as these reached the end of their lives, they were to be replaced by Andover C1s configured for reconnaissance. The intention was to convert a pair of Andovers, XS596 and XS641, to the role by fitting a suite of cameras and a false passenger compartment in the rear fuselage! The first of these 'PR' Andovers, XS596, was delivered in mid-1989, just in time for the fall of the Berlin Wall in 1989 and the end of the Cold War in 1991.

In the new world order of the post-Cold War era, the Treaty on Open Skies was signed, enabling designated unarmed reconnaissance aircraft to overfly the signatories' territories to permit monitoring of weapons status. Britain's aircraft was Andover C1(PR) XS596!

Andover C1(PR) XS641 was one of two examples converted to the photographic reconnaissance role in the last two years of the Cold War. The type continued in the role as Britain's platform for overflights under the Treaty on Open Skies. (Blue Envoy Collection)

Chapter 7
Trooping

The VC10 in particular was, and still is, a wonderful aeroplane …
Group Captain Marcus Wills, seminar on RAF Transports,
RAF Historical Society Journal, issue 22, 2000

From the start of World War Two, air links had been maintained across Africa and the Middle East, connecting the empire's outposts to the UK. From late 1944, Avro Yorks had carried troops to India and, by the 1950s, the trooping role, moving personnel where and when it was required, became more important. The Air Staff, in 1952, issued a requirement, OR.315, and Specification C.132 for a long-range high-speed personnel and light-stores transport aircraft.

The requirement was to move a Canberra wing and support personnel to Singapore, something the existing Hastings and Valetta fleet could not do with any degree of haste. Companies produced design studies based on the V-bombers, such as Avro submitting the Type 718, Handley Page the HP.96 and Vickers the Type 716. De Havilland drew up a modified Comet, while Short combined a new fuselage with the wings and tail of the Sperrin. None of these were deemed satisfactory and so were dismissed, with the companies advised to re-examine their designs, as the requirement now called for the aircraft to support the V-bombers.

The VC10 looks glorious from any angle, especially in the original RAF Transport Command scheme. Rather than being given an official name, each VC10 C1 was named after a holder of the Victoria Cross. In the case of XR810, the aircraft was named after David Lord VC, a Dakota pilot. (Blue Envoy Collection)

Vickers designed the V.1000 as a long-range high-speed transport to support V-bomber operations. The 1952 specification C.132 outlined a type with the performance that less than five years before would be challenging for a fighter aircraft. It was beyond the technology of the time. (Blue Envoy Collection)

Vickers responded with the V.1000, powered by four Rolls-Royce Conway engines, while de Havilland responded with the Comet 5. The Comet 5 was deemed unsuitable due to its cabin size and de Havilland's ongoing problems with the Comet's structure. Vickers did not have plain sailing with the V.1000. It suffered from weight gain, which in turn affected the aircraft's performance. In reality the V.1000 was a 'great leap forward' for a large aircraft, as the requirement was demanding performance that, until a couple of years before, had been the domain of the jet fighter.

Bristol via Belfast

The V.1000 was cancelled on 27 July 1955, as it was showing no sign of meeting the very demanding specification, especially take-off performance. The Air Staff and Air Ministry had already examined a Bristol Aircraft project for a turboprop-powered airliner aimed at transatlantic routes and opted for that instead of the now defunct V.1000. The Bristol 175 took to the air in August 1952 and soon became named the Britannia 100. For freight operations a fuselage stretch that involved a 6ft 8in (2.06m) extension forward of the wing and a 3ft 5in (1.04m) plug added aft. The new forward fuselage section incorporated an upward-opening cargo door on the port side, which allowed large items to be loaded, creating the Britannia 200, with a 'combi' version being designated Britannia 250.

Short in Belfast had been contracted to design and fit the reinforced floor for the Britannia freighter and finish off the aircraft for BOAC. The MoS let a contract to Short to produce three Britannia 252s for leasing and to use for trooping. Following the demise of OR.315/C.132 the RAF would be left without the trooper/transport they desperately needed so an order was placed for 20 Britannia 253s with full-length strengthened floors to meet Specification C.176/OR.276. These entered RAF service as the Britannia C1, with the first example entering service in June 1959. The original three Britannia 252s were taken into RAF service as the C2.

The RAF's first Series 252 Britannia C1 was delivered in June 1959 and the RAF's 20 C1s and three C2 Britannias served with 99 and 511 Sqn, carrying out the strategic transport role in support of operations around the shrinking British Empire in the 1960s. One operation where the reinforced floor and large cargo door proved its worth was the Zambian Oil Lift of 1965–66, a side-effect of Rhodesia's Unilateral Declaration of Independence in 1965. The Oil Lift was operated from Dar es Salaam in Tanzania to Lusaka in Zambia by six Transport Command Britannias alongside Royal Canadian Air

Right: A normal, busy day at RAF Lyneham. Transport Command Britannia C1s are being loaded while, in the background, are three Britannias, a Comet and a Hastings. (Bristol via Terry Panopalis)

Below: The RAF Transport Command's 20 Britannia 253s came with a large freight door and a strengthened cabin floor. Judging by the men in white coveralls, this Britannia is undergoing tests with a 25-pdr field gun and an Austin Champ light truck on the purpose-designed cargo lift. (Blue Envoy Collection)

Force and civilian aircraft. The Britannias could carry up to 56 44-gallon (200 litre) drums of fuel and oil, but the steel drums took their toll on the aircraft's flooring.

As British commitments East of Suez diminished, followed by the intended withdrawal from Malta, the Britannias, like the Belfasts, were deemed surplus to requirements. The 1975 Defence Review earmarked the Britannias for retirement from RAF service and, by the end of 1975, the 'Whispering Giant' had left the RAF. One former BOAC Britannia 312F, XX367, flew with the A&AEE and, like many of the former RAF Britannia freighters, ended its days flying cargo in central Africa.

High Speed Cast-Off

The British aviation industry has, since World War Two, made many attempts to steal a march on its American rivals, BAC's TSR.2 and Armstrong Whitworth's AW.681 being prime examples of this. One of the earliest endeavours in this involved civil air transport in the shape of the Brabazon Type IV.

The Brabazon Committee was set up in 1942 to identify aircraft types that could be used to connect the empire in a post-war world. The fear was that since the UK had concentrated on developing and building military aircraft, the US had a clear field in the transport stakes. This had been clear before the war when the US was developing the Douglas DC-3, DC-4 and Lockheed L-044 Excalibur (which led to the L-049 Constellation). In fairness, the British had, since 1938, been focused on fighters and bombers to the detriment of transport development.

The Brabazon Committee's interim report identified four main types, but, by 1943, the turbojet was seen as a viable alternative to the piston engine and at the insistence of Geoffrey de Havilland, a fifth type was added. The final report listed five types, with the Type II and Type V including two subtypes, while the added type, the Type IV, a 'high-speed mail-carrying airliner, gas-turbine powered', was intended to beat the Americans in the high-speed airliner field. The Air Ministry issued Specification 22/46 to cover development of this new jet aircraft, and this was issued to the companies in 1946, with submissions from Westland Aircraft and, of course, de Havilland.

The result was the de Havilland DH.106 Comet 1, the first jet airliner to enter service, powered by de Havilland Ghost turbojets and providing the technological leap its supporters hoped for. This achievement has since become overshadowed by the 'Comet Disaster'. This is not the place to examine this in detail, but suffice to say the airframe was reworked to have a reinforced structure, while the Ghosts were replaced with Rolls-Royce Avon turbojets to produce the Comet 2.

BOAC ordered 12 Comet 2s, but these lacked the range for the North Atlantic routes, so ten of these were passed on to the RAF, eight becoming the Comet C2, with two examples being used as training aircraft as the T2. A further three Comets were acquired for electronic intelligence gathering as the Comet 2R. These had not been reworked to Comet 2 standard and operated unpressurised with the crews wearing oxygen masks throughout their missions.

RAF Transport Command spanned the Earth and Comet C2 XK670 even got to Moscow. It is possibly on a diplomatic mission to the Soviet capital. In addition to trooping flights, Comets carried VIPs and delegations to conferences. (Blue Envoy Collection)

Not all of the RAF's Comet fleet operated as transports. Three Comet C2s were converted to the electronic intelligence gathering role as the Comet 2R. One of the three, XK633, was destroyed in a fire, so XK655 was acquired to replace it. The last Comet 2R was retired in 1975, replaced by the Nimrod R1. (Blue Envoy Collection)

The first of the Comet T2s, XK699 (ex-BOAC G-AMXB), entered service with 216 Sqn in early 1956, while the first of eight Comet C2s, XK655 (ex-G-AMXA, later converted to a 2R), arrived in late 1956. These were soon operating mainly in the high-speed transport and trooping roles, but they also conducted VIP and medical evacuation missions. As with the Britannias, the floor was reinforced, but a large cargo door was never fitted. The T2s were later converted to C2 standard and the C2 fleet operated as high-speed transports from the UK to the British bases East of Suez.

In what is possibly the first example of the now standard fuselage stretch on jetliners, the original Comet 1 fuselage was stretched by 18ft 6in (5.6m) to produce the Comet 4. This higher capacity and longer-ranged type attracted the Air Staff's attention, who in January 1960 issued Specification C.212 to cover the procurement of the Comet 4 as the Comet C4, with five examples ordered in September 1960. The first Comet C4 arrived on the strength of 216 Sqn at RAF Lyneham in June 1962.

A fine portrait of the de Havilland Comet C4's fine lines. Five examples joined the Comet C2 fleet operated by 216 Sqn, while a number of examples were operated by research establishments, such as the Royal Aircraft Establishment. The last two Comet 4Cs off the production line became the prototype Nimrod. (Blue Envoy Collection)

The 1975 Defence White Paper prompted the retirement of entire fleets of the RAF's transport aircraft, including the Comets. The C2s mainly went for scrap but the C4s, with relatively low hours, found their way into airline service with Dan-Air. A few Comet 4s were operated by the Royal Aircraft Establishment, while XS235 Canopus was operated by the A&AEE in various roles until it was retired. Comet 4s, XV147 and XV148, were the last Comets built and were used for Nimrod development, with XV147 becoming the Nimrod systems prototype, while XV148 was the aerodynamic development aircraft and fitted with Rolls-Royce Spey engines. During late 1976, XW626 was modified with a large nose radome as a test bed for the ill-fated Nimrod AEW3 programme. The last flight of a Comet anywhere was by XS235 *Canopus* when it was delivered to Bruntingthorpe in 1997. *Canopus* is maintained in flyable condition and performs on 'taxi days' at the Leicestershire airfield.

Queen of the Skies

The third type that grew from the need to support the British presence East of Suez had a long, distinguished and varied career for a type that could truly be described as the 'Queen of the Skies'. The majestic Vickers VC10 served in RAF colours for almost half a century, and its like will not be seen again. Intended for BOAC to service routes around the empire, the VC10 was required to operate from short, hot and high fields. As such it had plenty of power, high-lift devices on the wings and thrust reversers on two engines. Its undoing proved to be concrete as the short runways were soon extended to allow run-of-the-mill Boeing 707s to operate on the same routes.

The VC10's procurement followed the by-now standard long and winding road between proposal to delivery as the original specification C.213 was issued in January 1961. An order for five airline-standard Type 1100 VC10s was placed the following September.

A revised Specification C.239/ASR.378 was issued in December 1962 covering the Type 1106 VC10s fitted with a 12ft x 7ft (3.66m x2.1m) freight door on the port side of the forward fuselage. The original order for five Type 1100s was changed to 11 Type 1106s, and subsequently increased to 14 Type 1106s

The RAF's VC10 C1 was derived from the Vickers Type 1103, such as G-ASIW supplied to British United Airways. This model featured a large freight door. The type was exhibited at the Farnborough Airshow and the Rolls-Royce belonging to Freddie Laker, BUA's chairman, can be seen in the cabin. (Blue Envoy Collection)

in July 1964. The Type 1106 was derived from the Type 1103 with freight door, plus the Rolls-Royce Conway R.Co.43 engines and tail fin, with fuel tank, from the Super VC10.

The Type 1106 entered service in 1966 as the VC10 C1, serving in the trooping, passenger, light freight and medical evacuation roles. Two were also configured for the VIP role. By the time they entered service, their intended role of support for British outposts in the Middle and Far East had all but disappeared.

The VC10 C1s continued in service, and in the mid-1980s, the two Brize Norton-based transport squadrons that were equipped with the VC10 C1 were joined by a fleet of ex-airlines VC10s to meet Specification K.294/ASR.406. This fleet comprised five VC10 K2 Type 1112 inflight refuelling tankers converted from the Type 1101 Standard VC10 and four VC10 K3 Type 1164 tankers based on the Type 1150 Super VC10. The VC10 fleet was further expanded in the 1990s, when four VC10 K4 Type 1170s based on the Type 1151 entered service to meet Specification 415. With the heavier workload on tankers from 1990 and into the 21st century, ASR.416 was issued to cover fitting the VC10 C1 fleet with Flight Refuelling Ltd Mk.32 refuelling pods to become VC10 C1(K)s.

The VC10s remained in service until 2013, when they were replaced by the Airbus A330 Voyager. Interestingly, Voyager was one of the names suggested for the VC10 prior to its service entry in 1966. Rather than give the type a service name, the Air Staff opted to name each of the 14 VC10 C1s after RAF recipients of the Victoria Cross.

Named after Arthur Scarf VC, XV109 became a VC10 C1K tanker/transport after conversion in 1993. Like most of the VC10 C1 fleet, XV109 was repainted in 2005 and ended its career in Barley Grey but is seen here in its original white over grey. (Blue Envoy Collection)

Chapter 8

Communications

No real replacement has ever been found.

A. J. Jackson on the Dragon Rapide, *De Havilland Aircraft Since 1909*, Putnam, 1987

Variants of civil aircraft were used for communications duties in the interwar RAF, but one that went from pressed to procured service was the de Havilland DH.89 Dragon Rapide. The Rapide (as it was usually called) first flew in 1934 and was in service with several airlines, companies and a few private owners in the years running up to World War Two. On the outbreak of hostilities, these, like the other civil aircraft, were pressed into service with the military as radio operator training (Dominie I) or light transports/communications aircraft (Dominie II).

Supporting the V-Force was the Basset's initial role, but on the loss of the deterrent role, they faded away, sold off to the civil market or, in the case of XS743, converted to CC2 standard and used by the Empire Test Pilots' School (ETPS). Here, Basset XS743 is just prior to conversion and repainting in ETPS colours. (Via Phil Butler)

The de Havilland Dominie was used for communications flights throughout the war. This example, THA, was used by RAF Halton Station Flight. (Via Vic Flintham)

The Rapides were well-suited to these roles, so the Air Ministry ordered more. Hundreds more. As ever, the DH.89s for the RAF were renamed and given their role in training; they became known as Dominies, a Scots word for a teacher or mentor. Dominies, like most transport aircraft during wartime, were used as ambulances to carry the wounded and after the war, RAF Dominies carried severely ill civilians to hospitals for specialist treatment. This role continues into modern times, with RAF aircraft being used in the medevac role in support of the civil authorities.

Originally developed as an anti-submarine aircraft, the Avro 652 Anson soon attracted the Air Ministry's attention for other roles, which included training, so Specification 18/35 was issued, with the type entering service in 1936. Oddly enough, the Anson did not fare very well in its intended anti-submarine role, so was replaced by the Lockheed Hudson, which in turn led to the Anson mainly being used to train aircrew, at which it excelled. The Anson soon found another role as a ferry aircraft with the Air Transport Auxiliary, moving crews around the UK between aircraft factories and airfields. The RAF also used the Anson C.19 and C.21 for communications and light transport throughout the war and beyond, with the T22 radio trainer being the last variant to enter service. The last Anson operated by the RAF, as a communications aircraft, was finally retired in 1968.

Right: Dominies were operated as ambulance aircraft and could carry stretcher cases, although loading could be problematic. This Dominie carries 'invasion stripes', dating the photo to after 6 June 1944. (Via Vic Flintham)

Below: The RAF is still used for medical transfers in support of the civil authorities. Atlases are used for medical evacuation or transport of civilian patients. Airbus Atlas ZM403 is about to depart Aberdeen Airport, having carried a critically ill patient from the Orkney Islands for treatment at Aberdeen Royal Infirmary. (Author)

After the war, the RAF had a need to replace many of the civil passenger aircraft, Dominies and Ansons that it had used for communications work. De Havilland at Hatfield had started development of a light twin-engined airliner in 1943, and this gained further impetus from the recommendation of the Brabazon Committee and the need for an eight-seat twin-engined machine, identified as the Brabazon Type VB. The result was the de Havilland DH.104 Dove, which first took to the air six weeks after the war ended. Powered by a pair of de Havilland Gipsy Queen 70 engines, rated at 340hp (250kW) and capable of carrying eight passengers, the Dove became a successful small transport and airliner in military and civil service.

The RAF procured 39 examples of the Dove 4, which it promptly renamed Devon C1, while the Devon C2 was essentially a C1 re-engined with Gipsy Queen 175, rated at 400hp (300kW). The type was used by the various Communications Squadrons around the UK for VIP transport but was also occasionally used by The Queen's Flight.

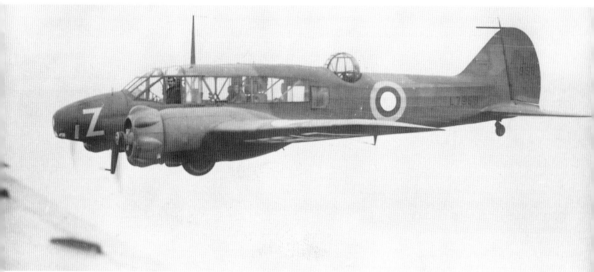

Ansons gave sterling service in the RAF and other allied air forces before, during and after the war. This Anson I, L7956Z, retains its turret and was probably photographed around 1939. (Via Vic Flintham)

Twenty years on, the Anson was still in RAF service, with Anson C21 WD415 being operated on communications duties by the Station Flight at RAF Chivenor in 1959. (Via Vic Flintham)

Pembroke

Another light transport serving with the RAF in the immediate post-war period was the Percival P.66 Pembroke. The Percival P.66 was acquired to meet specification C.121/OR.300 for a light transport and liaison aircraft for the RAF, which designated it as the Pembroke C1. It was derived from the civilian Percival Prince airliner and the Royal Navy's Sea Prince C2 but was fitted with wings that were extended by 8ft 6in (2.6m) to span 64ft 6in (19.66m). The Pembroke was to replace the Avro Anson and DH Devon in RAF service, with 27 being ordered in June 1951 and entering service in 1953. Fifty examples were ultimately acquired, six of which were C(PR)1 photo-reconnaissance variants that operated with 81 sqn in Malaya. A pair of Pembroke C1s were subsequently converted to C(PR)1 standard, bringing the number available to eight.

In the communications role, the Pembroke served around the world, including with the Metropolitan Communications Squadron, which later became 32 Sqn. The Pembrokes were mostly replaced by the Hawker Siddeley Andover CC2 in the mid-1960s, but the last C1s soldiered on with 60 Sqn in West Germany until 1988. Ostensibly used for communications flights to and from West Berlin, these Pembrokes were engaged in Operation *Hallmark*, which involved photographing Soviet and East German installations and equipment as the Pembrokes flew along the air corridors to West Berlin. These clandestine missions provided a great deal of intelligence on the Group of Soviet Forces in Germany and the East German *Nationale Volksarmee* order of battle in East Germany. The Pembrokes were replaced by more capable Andovers in 1989, but the fall of the Berlin Wall meant these were no longer required.

Percival's Pembroke served as a light transport and communications aircraft from the mid-1950s until the 1980s. Pembroke XV701 of 60 Sqn was operated from Wildenrath in West Germany. The Pembrokes of 60 Sqn were engaged in clandestine reconnaissance operations as they flew back and forth along the West Berlin air corridors. (Blue Envoy Collection)

Bassets for the V-Force

When the V-bombers were entering service as Britain's nuclear deterrent carriers, to reduce the possibility of a Soviet ballistic-missile strike destroying them on their home bases, the intention was to disperse them around the UK. To move crew around the dispersed sites, the Air Staff decided an aircraft was the ideal way to move aircrew. So, in September 1962 it issued Specification C.238 and ASR.372 for a small communications landplane, with an updated Spec. issued in October the following year. The requirement was to carry a fully kitted five-man V-bomber crew and one ground crew from a base in the UK to Malta.

Beagle Aircraft Ltd responded with a variant of the B.206, a twin-engined, seven-seater type, which it designated the B.206R, while the RAF called it the Basset CC1. The first of 20 Bassets for the RAF flew in December 1964 with the first entering service with the Northern Communication Squadron (subsequently redesignated as 26 Sqn) in 1965. By the time they entered service, the V-Force's days as a deterrent carrier were numbered. The role transferred to the Royal Navy in 1969, essentially meaning there was no role for the Basset.

The Bassets also served with The Queen's Flight, 32 (The Royal) Squadron; 207 Sqn (known as the Southern, then Strike Command Communications Squadron); and the Empire Test Pilots' School. In service, the Basset proved unreliable, and most were retired by the middle of 1974, subsequently sold off to the civil market.

Communications flying is still a key role for the RAF's transport fleet and became particularly important in the last three decades as the country's armed forces were engaged in Iraq and Afghanistan. VIP flying has also gained attention, with the seemingly never-ending round of summits and conferences to be attended by government ministers, officials and, of course, the Royal Family.

The Beagle Basset CC1 was intended to support the V-Force by transporting crews to dispersed sites around the UK and as far afield as Malta. With the acquisition of the Polaris system, the V-Force's role changed, and the Beagle fleet was no longer required. The Beagles were sold off, but a few were retained for trials, training and communications duties. (Via Phil Butler)

Chapter 9
The Only Logical Solution

Could it have been the best decision Harold Wilson ever made?
Wing Commander Paul Oborn, *RAF Historical Society Journal*, issue 22, 2000

Today, after more than 50 years in RAF service, for a modern observer the Hercules must have the only game in town when it came to buying a tactical transport aircraft. The origins of the Hercules in the RAF lie with Operational Requirement OR.351 for a tactical transport aircraft to replace the Beverley and be used for airborne assaults from Mounting Bases. The type would combine the carrying capacity of the Beverley, specifically the 10ft x 10ft (3.05m x 3.05m) hold cross-section. The first type selected to meet OR.351 was Armstrong Whitworth's AW.681, which used Bristol Pegasus or Rolls-Royce Medway engines with vectored thrust and boundary layer control (BLC) to provide STOL performance. Of note in relation to the AW.681 is that a VTOL variant used a completely new wing with 12 lift jets in each of its two wing pods and the BLC ducting used for reaction control systems. The two variants used completely different wings. Such was the complexity and potential expense of the AW.681 that it was cancelled in 1965.

The other type considered was the British Aircraft Corporation's BAC.222, a fascinating variant of the existing Lockheed C-130 Hercules. For the BAC.222, BAC at Filton took the Hercules, replaced the T56 turboprops with Rolls-Royce Tynes and remanufactured the wings and empennage to include BLC. All fairly straight forward, an engine upgrade and blown flaps. However, to meet OR.351 the fuselage was split horizontally and a 11in (28cm) section was inserted to produce a hold with a 10ft x 10ft (3.05m x 3.05m) cross-section. This aspect of the requirement dated back to the Air Staff's diktat on army equipment size. Hold size caused problems for all the bids OR.351. They were either too big,

The RAF has operated the C-130J since 1999, when the first C4 was delivered. They are due to be retired in 2023, with the Atlas replacing the type. Hercules C4 XH874 makes a low-level pass through LFA7, the tactical training area in west Wales. (Peter Edwards)

A model of the Armstrong Whitworth AW.681 that would have replaced the Beverley in the tactical transport role. The AW.681 was cancelled in 1965 and the C-130K procured. Whether it could have carried the Centurion tank on the right is debatable. (Blue Envoy Collection)

in the case of Handley Page HP.123 and Short Tactical Belfast, or too small, in the case of the C-130. The standard Lockheed C-130 had also been dismissed by the Air Ministry on the grounds it could not meet the required payload/range performance.

The AW.681 suffered the same fate as its more famous siblings in the 'Big Three': the BAC TSR.2 and Hawker P.1154 for the RAF were cancelled, ostensibly on costs grounds but in reality, aside from the P.1154, their roles no longer existed in a British defence posture that was oriented to the NATO Central Front and the eastern North Atlantic. To replace the Big Three, Denis Healey, Secretary of State for Defence, sought replacements in the US. The Royal Navy had already opted for the F-4K Phantom as its carrier-borne fighter in lieu of the P.1154, so it made sense to replace the RAF's version of the P.1154 with a Phantom, the F-4M. The General Dynamics F-111K was ordered to replace the cancelled TSR.2, but it did not reach flight status never mind enter service.

This brings us to the C-130. The Hercules can trace its lineage back to a USAF requirement issued in February 1951, with the aircraft entering service in 1956. The Air Staff was aware the AW.681 could face problems during development and was probably too ambitious for the state of the art in aircraft technology at the time. By early 1964, Assistant Chief of the Air Staff responsible for Operational Requirements (ACAS(OR)) Air Vice-Marshal Reginald Emson had set Group Captain O'Neil to the task of examining the case for the C-130E. O'Neil delivered his verdict in November 1964 and advised that the C-130 would be adequate for the role, but more would be needed, thanks to its smaller hold size compared with the AW.681.

Three months later, the AW.681 was cancelled and, despite a rear-guard action to simplify the type by fitting a Comet wing, the C-130 looked a better bet. The C-130 was not exempt from redesign by the British, who had already had a go with the BAC.222, but one last attempt was made to fit Tynes to the British Hercules to save on dollar expenditure. Rolls-Royce advised it was too busy with the Spey engines for the British Phantoms to take on a new project, so the Hercules was ordered pretty much off the shelf.

The first C-130K was essentially a C-130H fitted with British radios, a navigation kit and the British Air Delivery System used to safely release loads during parachute delivery. The first Hercules C1 was delivered in December 1966 to Marshall of Cambridge for the necessary modifications, and an 'East of Suez' dark stone and sand colour scheme was applied. The first Hercules was delivered to 36 Sqn in the summer of 1967. The 'Herks' were soon in action, airlifting personnel and equipment from Aden during the British withdrawal in December 1967.

By the mid-1970s, Britain's withdrawal from East of Suez was complete, and defence reviews saw the RAF's transport forces reduced, with the Belfast C1 and Britannia C1 fleets withdrawn as well as 13 Hercules C1s. Into the gap left by the Belfast stepped the Hercules, operating in a strategic 'trunk'

Right: A palletised load leaves the freight hold of a Hercules. A heavy load moving rapidly within the hold presents a problem to the pilots and a danger to the air loadmaster and crew. The C-130K was fitted with the British Air Delivery System that enabled large items to be despatched safely. Visible on the deck are the 'rollomat' panels that allow loads to move once released. (Blue Envoy Collection)

Below: The RAF's Hercules fleet was delivered to Marshall of Cambridge in bare metal for fitting out with British equipment and a sand and stone colour scheme. C-130K XV183 would later be 'stretched' to become a Hercules C3. (Terry Panopalis Collection)

Above: Another image that illustrates the British retreat from empire. Three Hercules C1s in the stone and sand scheme for East of Suez operations, XV196, XV205 and XV211, fly in formation with XV192, newly painted in the European grey/green scheme. (Blue Envoy Collection)

Left: Anyone attending British airshows in the 1970s would have been treated to the sight of a C-130K Hercules C1 making a dramatic 'Khe Sanh' STOL landing, rolling to a stop and a Scorpion reconnaissance vehicle being driven out of the hold. Hercules C1 XV293 still sports the stone and sand scheme applied to the type on delivery to the RAF in February 1968. (Blue Envoy Collection)

The difference between the Hercules C1 and the C3 is obvious. To address the cube limitation of the C-130K Hercules C1, Marshall of Cambridge was contracted to fit fuselage plugs forward and aft of the wings. Thirty Hercules C1s were converted to produce the C3. (Blue Envoy Collection)

role in addition to tactical tasks. This new role soon revealed that the Hercules 'bulked out' (also known as being 'cube limited'), as its stowage space was used up before it reached its weight limit. To address this, 30 Hercules C1s were stretched to C-130H-30 standard by Marshall of Cambridge who stretched the fuselage by 15ft (4.57m) with an 8ft 4in (2.54m) plug ahead of the wing box and a 6ft 8in (2.03m) plug aft of the wing. The stretch provided an increase in the cargo bay volume of 45 per cent, and on entering service in 1980, these stretched variants were designated Hercules C3.

In 1982, the Hercules fleet faced the new challenge of operating in support of British forces in the South Atlantic during the Falklands conflict. The Hercules C1 took on roles as diverse as tanker and VIP transport, while the C3 operated on trunk routes between the UK and Ascension Island. South Atlantic operations prompted the addition of a refuelling probe to 25 C1s to become C1Ps, while a tanker conversion saw a hose drum unit and drogue guides installed on a modified tail ramp with two or four modified Andover overload fuel tanks in the cabin to produce the C1(K). A total of six Hercules C1(K)s were delivered, and these performed admirably in support of other Hercules and, post-conflict, acted as tankers for the air defence Harriers and Phantoms on the Falklands until a new airfield was built at Mount Pleasant.

One Hercules was converted for weather research as the Hercules W2, featuring a long 'barber's pole' on the nose to carry sensors and keep these clear of airframe turbulence. The standard Hercules' nose radar was moved to a pod above the flight deck. The W2 conducted research for the UK Meteorological Office and other government agencies.

As a VIP aircraft, a Hercules C1P was used to carry Prime Minister Margaret Thatcher, her husband, Denis, and a few reporters to the Falkland Islands in January 1983. The prime minister travelled inside a specially fitted-out container in the Hercules' hold and the Hercules was refuelled in mid-air on the flights to and from the Falklands.

The Hercules was also used for weather research, with Hercules W2 XV208, fitted with sensors and workstations in the cabin to allow meteorological research to be conducted. Among the modifications was the new pod mounting above the cockpit for the APN-241 weather radar. On retirement from weather research, XV208 was used for trials of the TP400 engine for the Atlas. (Blue Envoy Collection)

Post-Falklands, the Hercules fleet worked hard and proved the transport force's maxim that they are always busy. In the mid-1980s, RAF Herculeses were involved in Operation *Bushel*, famine relief operations in Ethiopia and during the civil wars of the Balkans. The Hercules was pivotal to Operation *Cheshire* in support of the civilian population of the Bosnian city of Sarajevo.

By the late 1980s, preliminary work on a replacement for the Hercules was being carried out in Europe and the US. The Americans had examined a replacement for the C-130 in the mid-1970s under the Advanced Medium STOL Transport (AMST) programme, but neither of the projects that reached flight test, Boeing YC-14 and McDonnell Douglas YC-15, were procured. The upshot of that failed attempt to replace its star turn saw Lockheed returning to the drawing board and building a test bed for an improved Hercules.

First proposed for the Armstrong Whitworth Argosy in the late 1950s, what became the head-up display (HUD) finally reached the RAF's transport fleet in 1999, when the C-130J entered service. The HUD greatly aids low-level flight such as in the glens of the Scottish Highlands. (MOD/Open Government Licence)

The Hercules is more than a transport, and during the search for EgyptAir flight MS804, which had gone missing in May 2016. An air loadmaster conducts a visual search from the rear ramp of an Akrotiri-based RAF C-130J Hercules aircraft that took part in the Egyptian-led search and rescue operation. (MOD/Open Government Licence)

C-130K Hercules C1 XV181 was used as a testbed for the Rolls-Royce AE 2100 on the C-130J with its No.2 Allison T56 engine replaced by the AE 2100 engine, identifiable by its six-blade propeller. (Blue Envoy Collection)

The Lockheed High Technology Test Bed (HTTB) was based on a commercial L-100 and took to the air in 1984. It featured extended leading edges on the wings and modified control surfaces, including an extended chord rudder and ailerons, plus double-slotted flaps which, when combined with powered controls, improved the C-130's take-off and landing performance.

Lockheed was also one of the members of the Future International Military Airlifter (FIMA) group looking to develop a transport to replace the C-130, but it left the group in 1989. Lockheed applied many of the lessons from the HTTB and produced an updated Hercules, the C-130J. This was re-engined with Rolls-Royce AE2100 turboprops driving six-bladed propellors and a

Delivery of paratroops is still a role the RAF conducts, with regular exercises with the Parachute Regiment and its support troops. This Hercules C4 is delivering troops of the 16th Air Assault Brigade on an exercise on Salisbury Plain. The paratroops are using the Irving Low Level Parachute, which rapidly opens allowing lower altitude delivery of troops. (MOD/Open Government Licence)

Vickers Valentia

Handley Page Harrow

Bristol Bombay

Douglas Dakota

Avro York

Vickers Valetta C1

Handley Page Hastings C1

Blackburn Beverley C1

De Havilland Comet C2 and C4

Bristol Britannia C1 and C2

Armstrong Whitworth Argosy C1

Hawker Siddeley Andover C1

Shorts Belfast C1

Vickers VC10 C1

Lockheed Hercules C1

| 1940 | 1950 | 1960 | 1970 | 1980 |

The 1940s and '50s saw major advances in aircraft design and a plethora of types in service – eight in 1970 – but also reflects the changes in the UK's place in the world. The withdrawal of so many types in the mid-1970s illustrates this change – long-range trooping and strategic transports were no longer required. (Author)

new two-crew glass cockpit, complete with new avionics and modern systems that allowed a much-reduced crew workload. The cockpit also incorporated a HUD, as planned for the Argosy three decades before.

The RAF could not wait for a European solution to its Hercules replacement needs and, in 1996, became the launch customer for the C-130J, taking 15 of the stretched C-130J-30 as the C4 and 10 of the standard C-130J as the C5 with the first examples delivered in 1999. Like its predecessors, the Hercules C4 and C5 fleets were worked hard in the wars of the first two decades of the 21st century and, as of September 2021, are earmarked for retirement in 2023. However, the Hercules has been written off before.

The Long Wait for Atlas

The Hercules was operated by most of the NATO nations, sold well around the world and by the mid-1980s, like all transport aircraft, they had been worked hard. Air forces began to look at a replacement for their C-130 and C-160 Transall fleets and found the cupboard bare following the cancellation of the AMST programme in 1979. As might be imagined, the world's aircraft companies had been conducting design studies for a 'Hercules replacement' and the logical approach was to collaborate on a new design, rather than each company or country develop and build a new aircraft.

As ever, early in the process the countries all co-operated nicely, signed memoranda of understanding and discussed requirements for the Hercules replacement, and in 1982, Aérospatiale, BAe, Lockheed and Messerschmitt Bölkow Blohm (MBB) established the FIMA group. This soon produced two separate designs, FIMA A and FIMA B, and, of course, the consortium could not decide which to pursue. FIMA A was too big for the Europeans, while FIMA B was too small for the RAF and USAF. This situation led to FIMA D and FIMA E, with the E being split further!

FIMA disbanded in 1989, after Lockheed left to pursue the C-130J, but CASA of Spain and Aeritalia of Italy joined a new all-European consortium that was soon named Euroflag (European Future Large Aircraft Group) and set about designing a transport aircraft. In 1993, a European Staff Target was drawn up and issued followed by a European Staff Requirement in 1996.

With over 20 designs to choose from, selecting the powerplant should have been a straightforward decision – not so, this dragged on until turboprop power was selected in 1994, but unfortunately there was no engine available with the required power. The airframe design selected for development was Euroflag 36A, which would ultimately become the Airbus A400M – Atlas – while Europrop was established to develop the TP400 engine, rated at 11,000shp (8,200kW). As a service engine, its power is only exceeded by the Kuznetsov NK-12 that powers the Tupolev Tu-95 'Bear'.

A 'stractical' transport that can deliver loads over long distances and into austere airstrips, the Atlas is as at home in the valleys as it is at altitude. Atlas ZM416 demonstrates its agility as it powers through the Mach Loop in Wales. (Peter Edwards)

Disaster relief remains a regular task for the RAF's transport force into the 2020s. Atlas C1 XM414 of LXX Sqn was operating from Barbados during 2017's Operation *Ruman*, providing disaster relief for Caribbean islands hit by Hurricane Irma. (MOD/Open Government Licence)

After a protracted development that was rumoured to have almost bankrupted Airbus, the Atlas entered service with l'Armée de l'Air in September 2013, and, just over a year later, the RAF's LXX Squadron received its first Atlas C1, ZM400, in an official ceremony on 17 November 2014.

The Atlas C1 can carry up to 116 paratroopers and, in the medical evacuation role, up to 66 stretchers with 25 medical personnel. The capacious cargo compartment is 13ft 1in wide, 12ft 7in high and 58ft 1in long (4m x 3.85m x 17.7m) while the ramp provides a further 17ft 8in (5.4m) of usable space. It can carry a payload of up to 36.4 tons (37 tonnes) over a range of 2,000nm (3,704km) and deliver it into an austere airstrip.

Since entering RAF service, the Atlas has performed as intended and is particularly useful in the 'stractical' role, as its high-speed/high-altitude performance is almost on a par with jet transports,

The C-17A Globemaster, C-130J Hercules and A400M Atlas provide the RAF with a balanced transport force, especially when combined with the tanker/transport Voyagers and Chinook helicopters. (MOD/Open Government Licence)

Leaving a cloud of sand in its wake, Atlas C1 ZM414 powers into the air from a beach in south Wales. Atlas ZM414 was used for take-off and landing trials at the Pembrey Air Weapons Range in Wales during 2017 to prove the Atlas could operate from improvised runways. (MOD/Open Government Licence)

which makes it perfect on trunk routes. Perhaps the Atlas' finest hour in its career to date was the Kabul airlift of August 2021 with Atlases carrying refugees between Kabul's Hamid Karzai International Airport and Dubai in the Persian Gulf before transferring to Airbus Voyagers for onward flights to Brize Norton in the UK.

Stractical Transport

Within six years of the Belfast's retirement, a situation arose in the South Atlantic that worked the RAF's support fleet of transports and tankers harder than the Air Staff ever imagined. Supporting Operation *Corporate* revealed a gap in the RAF's transport needs – a large capacity strategic machine. The Belfasts that were in commercial service with HeavyLift were roped in to provide airlift of items to Ascension Island. Eight years on from *Corporate*, the movement of materiel to Saudi Arabia and Bahrain in support of Operation *Granby* also required the use of civil-operated Belfasts or USAF C-5 Galaxies, if available. Into the 1990s, Britain's armed forces became involved in operations in places as diverse as the Balkans and West Africa. The MOD turned east for its outsized transport requirements, chartering Antonov An-124 'Condors' operated by Air Foyle/Antonov, which prompted a review of the RAF's airlift needs. This soon became the Short-Term Strategic Airlift (STSA) requirement, as proposed in the 1998 Defence White Paper. The STSA requirement was very much a modernised version of the requirement that led to the Belfast: move a rapid reaction force over 3,200 miles (2,781nm/5,150km) within seven days.

The experience of Operation *Corporate* and the expansion of British operations around the world in the 1990s raised the requirement for strategic transport aircraft. The RAF took delivery of its first Boeing Globemaster (the RAF eschews the American number suffix) in 2001. Globemaster ZZ178 was the last of the eight examples to enter service with 99 Sqn in 2012. (MOD/Open Government Licence)

Transport carries transport. A Chinook HC6 loaded in a 99 Sqn Globemaster ready for a flight to Oman to take part in Exercise *Saif Sareea 3*. (MOD/Open Government Licence)

Tenders were invited, with three bids: the standard An-124 from Antonov, an 'Anglicised' An-124 with Rolls-Royce engines and Western avionics from Air Foyle and the Boeing C-17A Globemaster III, which was the Air Staff's preference. Unfortunately, the entire process was scrapped, as the first proposal was deemed susceptible to political instability in the former Soviet Union, the second fraught with technical problems from integration and the last bid too expensive according to HM Treasury. However, the MOD convinced the Treasury that the C-17 was the best value and after some negotiations with Boeing, an agreement to lease four C-17s was drawn up and the first of these Globemaster IIIs was delivered in May 2001, with the fourth arriving at Brize Norton in August 2001. The type has been very successful in RAF service, and in 2004, the MOD bought the four leased examples and ordered more, ultimately acquiring eight examples by 2012, all operated by 99 Sqn. Since the Globemasters were originally leased, they were not assigned an RAF designation, which technically should have been Globemaster C1.

The C-17's cargo compartment is 18ft wide, 14ft 9in high and 68ft 2in long (5.5m x 4.5m x 20.8m) and can accommodate just about any item of equipment used by the British Army. Due to operational commitments the C-17, like its Belfast predecessor, was not cleared for parachuting, air drops or rough field operations, as no aircraft could be spared for the three years such trials would have taken. This means that the C-17 is used by the RAF in the strategic role, rather than the 'stractical' role the USAF can use its fleet of Globemasters for, i.e. flying equipment directly into forward bases from their home stations.

The Globemasters of 99 Sqn have been heavily used for the last 20 years, in support of operations in Iraq and Afghanistan, being particularly busy during Operation *Pitting*, the Kabul airlift of August

Moving helicopters is yet another task at which the Globemaster excels. This Puma HC2 is one of two that have been prepared for transport and loaded into a C-17 for a flight to Oman for Exercise *Saif Sareea 3* in 2018. (MOD/Open Government Licence)

A 99 Sqn Globemaster being loaded with spares for a 240 Sqn Puma destined for the British Virgin Islands. The RAF helped provide disaster relief after Hurricane Irma hit the islands. Even with modern handling systems, some things have not changed since the days of the Vickers Vernon. (MOD/Open Government Licence)

2021. In addition to carrying troops and equipment, the Globemaster can be configured for casualty evacuation with what is effectively a flying intensive care unit. This capability has not only been used to return wounded troops from Iraq and Afghanistan but to repatriate civilians injured in terrorist attacks in Tunisia during 2015. The RAF's C-17 force has also been used in support of allies, including France during Operation *Serval* in Mali during 2013.

Britain's Extender

The Yom Kippur/October War of 1973 between Israel and neighbouring Arab states revealed a gap in the inventory of the USAF's transport fleet. Called upon to deliver materiel from the US to Israel and denied staging rights in western Europe, the only USAF transport that could be refuelled in flight was the Lockheed C-5A Galaxy, and these bore the brunt of the operation, known as Operation *Nickel Grass*. As a result, the soon-to-be stretched Lockheed C-141A Starlifters were also to be fitted with refuelling receptacles, but *Nickel Grass* also prompted development of a new class of transport aircraft: the tanker/transport.

The resulting McDonnell Douglas KC-10A Extender combined the freight capacity of the DC-10-30F civil cargo aircraft with a refuelling capability, as both receiver and tanker, with a hose drum unit (HDU) and Advanced Aerial Refuelling Boom under the rear fuselage and a boom receptacle above the cockpit. Around the same time in the 1970s, Hawker Siddeley began to examine a new design based on the Airbus A300 that could perform a multitude of tasks including airborne early warning, tanker, electronic reconnaissance, and, of course, transport. The Multi Role Support Aircraft (MRSA) was to replace a variety of RAF types and in 1981 the Air Staff drew up a requirement, ASR.411, for a tanker/transport aircraft that became known as the Super Tanker. Unfortunately, in 1981 there were no funds for the Super Tanker, but that soon changed in April 1982.

The Falklands conflict placed a heavy burden on the RAF's tanker and transport aircraft, with the Hercules and various chartered cargo aircraft, including the Belfasts the RAF had relinquished six years before, roped in to support operations in the South Atlantic. As a result, ASR.411 was pretty much resurrected as originally written. Interestingly, the RAF came to the same conclusion as the USAF and selected the McDonnell Douglas DC-10-30F. As luck would have it, several DC-10-30s from the recently collapsed Laker Airways were in storage and would be suitable for conversion to tanker transports.

The Thatcher government had other ideas, and a cash-strapped British Airways had to dispose of some of its fleet, including a few Lockheed L-1011 TriStars. Six L-1011-500 TriStars were purchased from British Airways in late 1982, while another three were acquired from Pan American Airways in 1984. All were converted to tankers by Marshalls of Cambridge to produce two passenger/tanker

'Perky' was the nickname applied to TriStar K1 ZD951 when it and the other K1 ZD949 (nicknamed 'Pinky') were finished in 'Desert Pink' for Operation *Granby* in 1990–91. They were named after a pair of puppets from the TV show *Pinky and Perky*. (Blue Envoy Collection)

TriStar K1s, four KC1 passenger or cargo/tanker aircraft and three passenger aircraft (two TriStar C2s and one TriStar C2A). These were fitted with a pair of HDUs under the rear fuselage, although the original K1s had a single HDU.

Following an interlude flying Buccaneers in West Germany, 216 Sqn, which had previously been equipped with the Comet C2 and C4, operated the nine TriStars from March 1986. The TriStar fleet supported UK and NATO operations around the world, mainly refuelling but also by conducted trooping flights in support of operations in the Falklands, Iraq and Afghanistan. The TriStars were withdrawn, and 216 Sqn disbanded in March 2014, with the Airbus A330 Voyager taking on the tanker/transport role, effectively the Super Tanker of 40 years ago.

With USAF KC-10 Extenders and RAF TriStars proving the concept of the wide-body airliner as military tanker/transport, more air forces adopted this class of aircraft. The Royal Canadian Air Force and the Luftwaffe adopted the Airbus A310 as the CC-150 Polaris and A310 MRTT (Multi Role Tanker Transport) respectively, but Airbus had much grander ideas based on the much larger A330.

For deployment of troops or other personnel, the Voyager fleet is ideal. A Voyager can carry up to 291 passengers (depending on internal configuration) and a maximum payload of just under 100,000lb (45,350kg). This Voyager KC3 has carried RAF personnel and equipment to Nellis AFB in Nevada for *Red Flag* exercises. In addition to moving personnel and kit, the Voyager would have refuelled the fighter aircraft en route and supported them during the exercise. (MOD/Open Government Licence)

Through a private finance initiative deal with AirTanker plc, the RAF effectively rents flight time on a fleet of 14 Airbus A330 MRTTs, known in the RAF as Voyagers, which interestingly had been suggested as a name for the Vickers VC10 back in the 1960s. Three Voyager KC2s, with Cobham 905E underwing refuelling pods and seven KC3s with pods and a Cobham 805E fuselage HDU, replaced the VC10s previously operated by 10 and 101 Sqns, while a further four Voyagers are held by AirTanker plc as a 'surge fleet' that can also be chartered to civil airlines. While the Voyagers mainly operate in the air-to-air refuelling role, they also undertake transport duties, with palletised freight in the lower holds. The type's first operation was a transport mission to Cyprus in May 2012.

Voyagers play a key role in the support of the Falkland Islands garrison, staging through Ascension Island or Dakar in Senegal, carrying personnel and stores to RAF Mount Pleasant. Voyagers carried evacuees onwards to Brize Norton in the UK, after being airlifted from Kabul to airports in the Gulf states on Globemasters and Atlases. One other high-profile role for a Voyager is carrying VIPs on official visits, with KC2 ZZ336 being fitted with a VIP interior and repainted during deep maintenance. A 2021 prime ministerial visit to the Falklands would be more comfortable than Mrs Thatcher's bumpy trip in the back of a Hercules in 1983.

Left: After almost five decades in RAF service, the VC10 was finally retired in September 2013 and replaced by the Airbus Voyager KC2 and KC3. Voyager ZZ331, operating with 10 Sqn, flies in formation with VC10 K3 ZA150 from 101 Sqn. VC10 ZA150 was originally a Super VC10 operated by East African Airways and the last VC10 built. (Geoffrey Lee via AirTanker Plc)

Below: The last 40 years have been dominated by the Hercules and the VC10, but as these reached the end of their serviceable lives, a new generation of modern transports took over, albeit that one was a Hercules! (Author)

			Hercules C1 and C3
	Hercules C4 and C5		
	VC10 C1, K2, K3 and K4		
	TriStar K1, KC1 and C2		
		Globemaster III	
		Voyager KC2 and KC3	
		Atlas C1	

| 1980 | 1990 | 2000 | 2010 | 2020 |

Chapter 10

Flying the Brass

The aircraft's new paint scheme will better reflect its prestige role which we are proud to undertake.
Air Commodore Simon Edwards, on delivery of VIP Voyager ZZ336 in its *Vespina* scheme

W hile not strictly a role for transport aircraft, flying members of the Royal Family dates to
1916 when the Prince of Wales, the future Edward VIII, took a flight over northern France.
The Royal Family remained interested in flying, with Prince Albert (future George VI)
joining the RAF in 1919. A pair of Westland Wapitis was ordered in 1928 for royal use and delivered to
24 Sqn, but it was the Prince of Wales who increased the Royal Family's interest in flying and aircraft.
The Prince of Wales gained his pilot's licence in 1929 and flew to many of his public engagements in
his own collection of aircraft that included a few de Havilland Moth variants. On his accession to the
throne in January 1936, Edward VIII became the first monarch to fly in an aircraft.

Through the 1920s and early 1930s, the RAF had a semi-official Royal Flight, with the Prince of
Wales being its most frequent user and effectively the operator of the Royal Flight. The flight included,
at various times, a Vickers Viastra, a DH Dragon and a Dragon Rapide, which was replaced by an
Airspeed AS.6J Envoy. Soon after Edward VIII's accession, the Royal Flight was made official as The
King's Flight and equipped with a range of aircraft.

The King's Flight was disbanded in 1942, but the Royal Family still flew in RAF aircraft, not only on
transports such as the de Havilland DH.96 Flamingo but, on occasion, on a pair of Lockheed Hudsons.
The latter type was the only armed aircraft to serve in The King's Flight and apparently the only time
a member of the Royal Family had flown in an armed aircraft until Prince Harry flew Apache attack

**A BAe 146 CC2 and two BAe 125 CC3s, ZD620 and ZE396, form up for the Queen's Jubilee flypast in 2002. The
BAe 146 serves in two guises, CC2 in the VVIP role, such as ZE700 seen here, and the C3 with a cargo door that
can be used in the light freight and passenger transport role. The C3 also has a medical evacuation role. (MOD/
Open Government Licence)**

helicopters in Afghanistan. For longer flights, such as journeys to North Africa, George VI used Winston Churchill's Avro York.

The King's Flight was re-instated in 1946, equipped with a de Havilland DH.89 Dominie along with some of the first Vickers VC.1 Viking airliners, two of which were fitted out as VIP aircraft for a royal tour of South Africa in 1947. Four Viking C2s were ordered, one for the King, one for the Queen and a third fitted out with 21 seats for accompanying dignitaries. The fourth machine was a mobile workshop carrying the support staff and their kit. An Avro York was used by the Duke of Gloucester during his service as Governor-General of Australia and was operated by the RAAF.

Renamed on the accession of Queen Elizabeth II in 1952, The Queen's Flight acquired new types in the shape of the de Havilland Dove, in which the Duke of Edinburgh learned to fly multi-engine aircraft, and the Heron. One DH Heron C3 was procured to meet Specification C.151P2 as a personal aircraft for the Duke of Edinburgh and another to meet C.151P3 for a Heron C(VVIP)4 to be used by The Queen's Flight. Another DH Heron was supplied to support the British Joint Services Mission in Washington, DC and was fitted with a VIP interior and 'special equipment' and was designated the Heron C3.

With global war underway by 1942, commanders needed to move around and between theatres, leading to a requirement for VIP aircraft. Dakotas were a favourite, having the interior space to carry generals, air vice-marshals or admirals and their staff. RAF top brass including Tedder, Leigh-Mallory and Air Chief Marshal Portal, Chief of the Air Staff, used a Douglas Dakota II (a C-53), TJ167, that sported a fetching Air Force blue colour scheme. General Montgomery used a Boeing B-17E until it was damaged beyond repair at Palermo in July 1943. Monty then acquired a series of Dakotas including a C-47 in USAAF colours but bearing the insignia of the Eighth Army and 21st Army Group on the nose. Lord Mountbatten, as Supreme Allied Commander South East Asia Command, also used Dakotas, most famously a USAAF C-47A 42-100536 'Hapgift' that had been 'gifted' by Commanding General of the USAAF 'Hap' Arnold. On the more localised scale, many commanders, including Tedder and Montgomery, used the Miles Messenger I, a single-engined, four-seat cabin monoplane design to meet Specification 17/43.

For long-range inter-theatre flights or for conferences such as Casablanca in January 1943, larger types with longer range were required to carry Allied leaders, their generals and their staff. Churchill's aircraft, a Liberator II called *Commando,* is probably the most famous

Commando and Beyond

Britain's prime ministers have used aircraft on numerous occasions, but these are rarely noticed by the general public. The first example was the Lockheed 14 Super Electra that carried Neville Chamberlain to and from his meeting with Hitler at Munich in 1938.

As mentioned in Chapter 3, Chamberlain's successor as prime minister, Winston Churchill, had a personal aircraft at his disposal. One of Churchill's first flights as prime minister was in a RAF de Havilland DH.95 Flamingo that carried him to and from his meeting near Tours with French Prime Minister Reynaud.

For his visits to troops in Egypt and meetings with generals and allies, Churchill, in July 1942, was given the use of a Consolidated Liberator II, AL504, which acquired the name *Commando* and was given a VIP interior. As the second Very Long-Range Liberator II delivered, *Commando* had the standard Liberator glazed nose and twin fins but was modified to have a longer, solid nose, the empennage from the Consolidated PBY-4 Privateer and windows added to the passenger compartment.

After using *Commando* to attend significant meetings, including the Casablanca Conference of January 1943 and carrying General Montgomery to his new command in Egypt, *Commando* was replaced by one of the Avro York prototypes, LV633, which was named *Ascalon*. The York was, in

Six de Havilland DH.95 Flamingos served with the RAF during the war and would carry Winston Churchill to his meetings with his French counterpart in May 1940. The Flamingo also served with The King's Flight. This example, G-AFYH, was used by the Royal Navy and was finally retired and scrapped in 1954. (Blue Envoy Collection)

turn, replaced by a Douglas C-54B Skymaster until this and the other nine C-54s in RAF service were returned under Lend-Lease rules.

After the war, Yorks continued to be used but were soon replaced by more modern types, and eventually the de Havilland Comet became the preferred type for long-range VIP trips with Doves and Devons used for shorter routes. June 1963 saw an order for six HS.748 Series 2 airliners for use as VIP transports to carry the RAF's senior staff and other VIPs. Then, in 1964, two HS.748s out of that order for six Andover CC2 VIP machines were converted to VVIP standard to meet Specification C.219 and entered service with The Queen's Flight to replace the DH Herons. These VVIP-configured variants of the HS.748 airliner, XS789 and XS790, served until December 1990. The replacement for the Andover was the BAe 146, configured to BAe's Statesman standard and designated BAe 146 CC2 in RAF service. Two examples fitted out for royal duties were delivered in 1986, with a third arriving in service during 1990. A further two BAe 146 C3s were operated by 32(TR) Sqn in the light freight and personnel transport role. The C3 has a freight door in on the port side, aft of the wing.

Another jet-powered type used by VIPs and government officials was the Dominie, the RAF's version of the Hawker Siddeley HS.125. This had been developed by de Havilland as the DH.125 Jet Dragon executive jet and, on the integration of de Havilland into Hawker Siddeley, its designation was changed to HS.125 and the Jet Dragon name dropped. The RAF adopted the HS.125 as an aircrew trainer designated Dominie T1. Further examples were procured for use in the VIP and communications roles as the HS.125 CC1 (based on the HS.125 Series 400) and the HS.125 CC2 (HS.125 Series 600) and the BAe 125 CC3 (BAe 125 Series 700). These served with 32 (The Royal) Sqn and mainly carried senior officers and government officials, while members of the Royal Family occasionally flew in the HS.125s until the type was retired in 2015.

The BAe 125 fleet did range further afield during their service, mainly used for intra-theatre communications. BAe 125 CC3 ZD740 was one of 12 RAF, Army Air Corps and Fleet Air Arm aircraft damaged by a freak hailstorm at Kandahar Airport in Afghanistan on 23 April 2013. The aircraft had been carrying VIPs on a visit to personnel serving in Afghanistan and had been operating from Kandahar. All the aircraft were inspected, repaired and returned to service apart from the BAe 125, as the damage was such that it had to be dismantled and flown back to the UK for assessment. It was subsequently struck off charge and now resides in the Cornwall Aviation Heritage Centre.

Above: As well as operating with 32 (The Royal) Sqn in the VIP role as the CC2, the BAe 146 C3 can be used for medical evacuation. The C3 has a large cargo door through which medical support equipment can be loaded. (MOD/Open Government Licence)

Right: The Queen's Flight and 32 (The Royal) Squadron have operated all over the world. This BAe 125 CC3, ZD704, sustained hail damage at Kandahar Airport in 2013. Some of the many dents caused by hail can be seen on the panel forward of the windscreen. (Author)

The Royal Family also used 'standard' RAF transport aircraft for longer flights, particularly the Comet and VC10, with two VC10s fitted for the VIP role and operated by 10 Sqn. Her Majesty The Queen also used commercial aircraft, including Concorde for visits, most notably to Barbados, where an example of the type is preserved.

Aside from Margaret Thatcher's trip to Port Stanley in a Hercules, flying by British prime ministers became a run-of-the-mill occurrence. Tony Blair tried to acquire a prime ministerial aircraft that inevitably earned the moniker 'Blairforce One', but despite funds for an aircraft, probably an Airbus A330, being allocated, the plan was scrapped by Gordon Brown when he became prime minister. David Cameron had similar plans but resigned before they came to fruition.

Enter Boris Force One

As foreign secretary, Boris Johnson had used the VIP configured Airbus Voyager KC3 ZZ336 on trips abroad. Boris was quite vocal in his belief that senior ministers, the prime minister and even Her Majesty The Queen did not look good arriving for a state visit in a Barley Grey colour-schemed tanker. On becoming prime minister, Boris was determined to change things, and ZZ336 received a new and rather spectacular paint job. All hell broke loose in the press about wasting money on 'Boris Force One' (one of the many less derogatory names applied by the tabloid press and public), but the VIP Voyager was given the new *Vespina* scheme during its deep maintenance and would have been repainted anyway. *Vespina* is the RAF codename for the VIP operations carried out by Voyager. It does look spectacular, and this author looks forward to seeing photographs of ZZ336, operating as the support tanker for RAF Typhoons, alongside a Russian 'Bear'.

Another Airbus type, an A321NeoLR, G-XATW, has been chartered from Titan Airways and given the *Vespina* colour scheme. The aircraft made its somewhat controversial debut flying the prime minister and his entourage from London Stansted to Newquay Airport in Cornwall for the G7 summit in June 2021.

RAF Voyager KC2 ZZ336 sports the Union Flag representing a 'Global Britain' on its *Vespina* role as a VIP aircraft. The aircraft in the background is A330 MRTT G-VYGJ, part of the Air Tanker plc 'surge' fleet. (MOD/open Government Licence)

Conclusion

Until the national lockdown of March 2020, most people in the UK had never noticed the RAF's transport aircraft going about their daily business. The grey Atlases or Globemasters and green Hercules had previously operated virtually unnoticed, but with most civil air traffic grounded, the RAF's transport aircraft made the newspapers and news websites, with headlines such as 'Giant military aircraft over city yesterday'. There was nothing new in this, they had always been there, moving equipment, transferring patients or training. Just another aircraft.

That pretty much sums up the RAF's transport operations: always busy doing something, in the background and generally something unexpected. Only the aircraft have changed in over a century, exemplified by the evacuation of Kabul in 1929 and again in 2021. Same mission, different aircraft. Never at peace.

Always busy but heading for home. A 99 Sqn Globemaster departs the Persian Gulf bound for Brize Norton. In over a century of operations, the RAF's transport force has conducted missions on a daily basis. The RAF in the second decade of the 21st Century boast one of the most capable transport fleets in the world. (MOD/Open Government Licence)

Glossary

Transport Command spanned the world in its 1960s heyday and operated a variety of British aircraft. Framed by the wing of an Armstrong Whitworth Argosy, a Blackburn Beverley, cargo doors agape, awaits a load. (Jet Heritage Museum via Tony Buttler)

A&AEE	Aircraft & Armament Experimental Establishment
AdlA	*Armée de l'Air* (French Air Force)
AMC	Air Mobility Command
ASR	Air Staff Requirement
AST	Air Staff Target
AWA	Armstrong Whitworth Aircraft
BEA	British European Airways
BOAC	British Overseas Airways Corporation
CASA	Construcciones Aeronáuticas SA
Casevac	Casualty Evacuation. Generally written in block capitals in military documents, but in lower case in this work for easier reading.
DUKE	Dominion, United Kingdom, Empire – armed forces of the British Empire operating during World War Two
ECM	Electronic Countermeasures
FSTA	Future Strategic Tanker Aircraft
HDU	Hose Drum Unit
MBB	Messerschmitt-Bölkow-Blohm
MRTT	Multi Role Tanker Transport
OR	Operational Requirement
RAAF	Royal Australian Air Force
RAE	Royal Aircraft Establishment
RAF	Royal Air Force
RCAF	Royal Canadian Air Force
RFC	Royal Flying Corps
SAL	Scottish Aviation Ltd
SAS	Special Air Service
SOE	Special Operations Executive
Sqn	Squadron
STOL	Short Take-off and Landing
Stractical	Describes an aircraft capable of operating into tactical landing strips over strategic range. The C-17 is a prime example.
Surge Fleet	Three (previously four) Voyagers used for civil charter work by AirTanker plc.
Truckie	RAF slang for a pilot of a transport aircraft

Select Bibliography

Books

Gibson, C, *On Atlas' Shoulders*, Crecy Publishing, 2016

Gibson, C, *Vickers VC10 – AEW, Pofflers and Other Unbuilt Variants*, Blue Envoy Press, 2009

Wynn, H, *Forged in War: History of RAF Transport Command, 1943-67*, OHMS, 1996

Cox, G and Kaston, C, *American Secret Projects 2: U.S. Airlifters 1941 to 1961*, Crecy Publishing, 2019

Cox, G, and Kaston, C, *American Secret Projects 3: U.S. Airlifters Since 1962*, Crecy Publishing, 2020

Journals

RAF Historical Society Journal, various issues

Flight International, various issues

Aeroplane, various issues